the Stone Walls

For John & Gladys

If you like it, spread the word (available on Amazon)

If you don't, Mum's the word.

Wishing you health & happiness

Bob.

Copyright © R. R. McCaskill with Nuru Patterson, 2016
Copyright © M.V. Russell, 2016

Published by M.V. Russell
All rights reserved

Illustrations by M. Sugranyes
Design by W. Wartena
Printed by Inky Little Fingers

ISBN 978-0-9955483-1-2

From Within the Stone Walls

R. R. McCaskill
with Nuru Patterson

London, 2016

Contents

Introduction	6
Prologue	12
Part One, The Kenya Years	17
Part Two, A Souvenir from Kenya	79
Epilogue	140

Introduction

For the most part, this is one story about the life of a Swahili lady, born Nur (Nuru in Swahili) Masoud Mohammed Muhashamy, but it is presented in two parts to reflect her own view of her life. Nuru's early years in Kenya are so distinct from the life she found in England, and later Barbados, that when talking of her younger life she still thinks in Swahili…whilst talking in English. Her children lovingly refer to the result as her 'Swahenglish". Placed on the page verbatim, it would not make for easy reading.

In addition to speaking about Nuru's childhood in Mombasa, and later Nairobi, Part one attempts to give a broader historical picture of Kenya before and during that time. Much of this content was not something Nuru thought about then and does not reflect upon now. For these reasons, the scene is set in Part one, 'The Kenya Years', as a narrative. In Part two, 'A Souvenir from Kenya', Nuru emerges as a young adult to tell her own story.

From the outset Nuru asked me to write the book because of the trust that exists between us. She decided that she must be able to talk about her whole life including aspects of it that she had never discussed with anyone before, including her ex-husband and children. This was an enormous leap of faith on her part and required a great deal of courage: not only did she need to be able to trust me with such confidences but this also meant that she must face demons that had remained buried for several years. Many tears were shed.

Throughout the years, countless people have told her that she must ask someone to write her story; they know only a fraction of what lies within the following pages. Nonetheless, each fragment had been sufficient for them to urge her on.

It was implicit from the very beginning that Nuru should be the final editor; I always insisted that she alone must decide what should and should not be included. This was not only for her own sake but also out of consideration for others who play an intrinsic role in the telling of her story.

In the final analysis, we agreed that some of her memories and experiences had no good reason to be aired. But this applied only where the content was incidental to the main body of the story and would serve only to hurt others.

The most courageous act was for Nuru to decide not to edit anything directly relating to herself and her experiences. She did not take that decision lightly. The result is a comprehensive account of her remarkable life so far.

Nuru assures me that the accuracy of the facts as they are portrayed is faithful to her memory of them as told to me during our long and often emotional sessions together.

I feel privileged to have been taken into her confidence and I hope I have treated her, sometimes-harrowing story, with the tenderness and respect it deserves.

R. R. McCaskill

Muhashamy and Abed partial family tree

Grandparents father's side

Salim & Nur Muhashamy
Salim Muhashamy
Said Muhashamy
Shamsa Muhashamy (aunt)
Masoud Muhashamy (Dad)

Masoud & Aziza
Husna, Nur (Nuru), Mohammed, Salma

Masoud & Rehema
Shahida & Rafiki

Aziza & Ahmed
Warda, Omar, Nasib, Mohammed, Yusriya, Fuad and Zahra

Introduction

Grandparents mother's side

Omar Abed & Mwan Mkaa
Abed, Tefle, Esha, Saida, Swalehe
Fatuma, Mwamadi, Maryam
Aziza (mother)
Gheda

Arabian Sea / Northern Indian Ocean

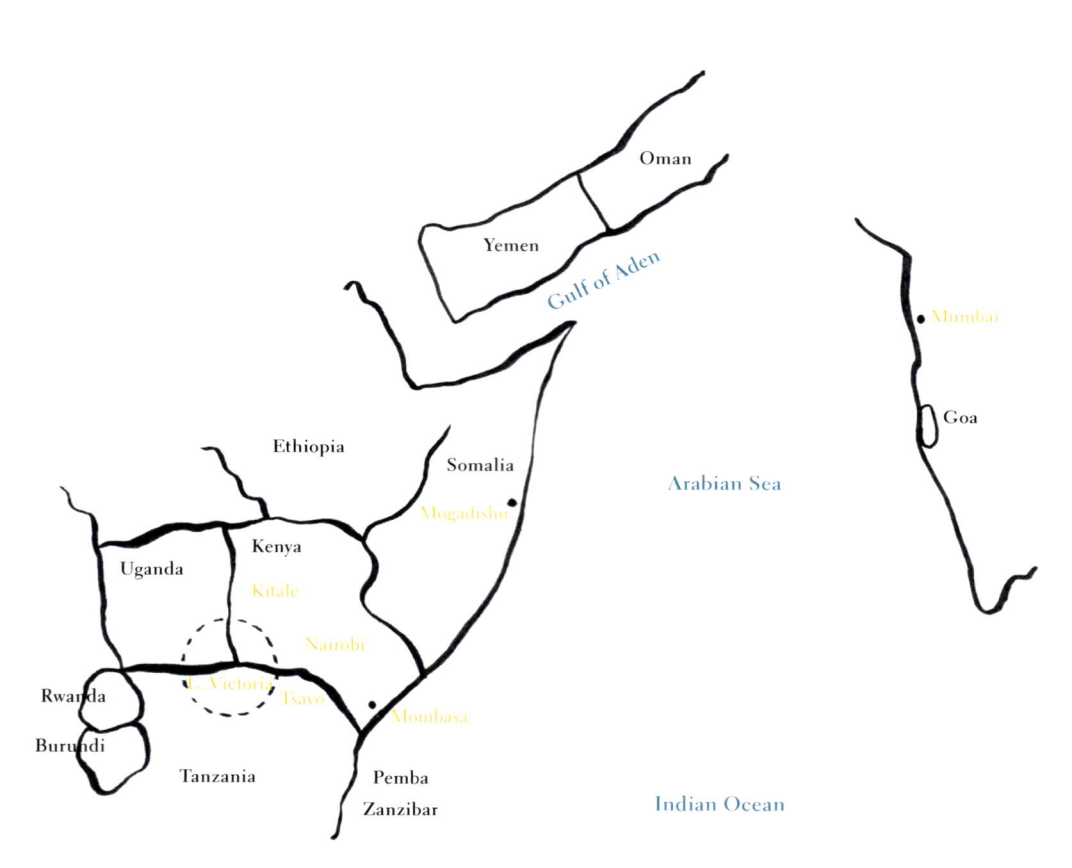

Introduction

Mombasa

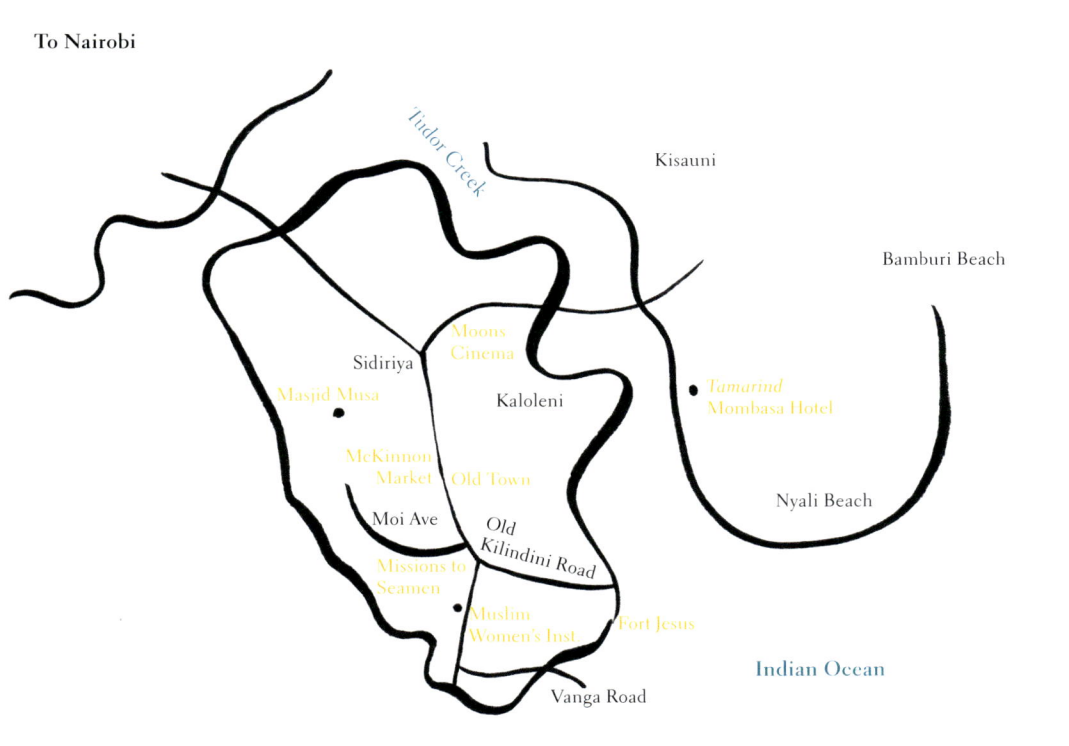

To Nairobi

Tudor Creek

Kisauni

Bamburi Beach

Moons Cinema

Sidiriya

Kaloleni

Tamarind Mombasa Hotel

Masjid Musa

McKinnon Market *Old Town*

Moi Ave

Old Kilindini Road

Nyali Beach

Missions to Seamen

Muslim Women's Inst. *Fort Jesus*

Vanga Road

Indian Ocean

11

Prologue

Despite much speculation, supported in the main by unconvincing evidence, there has been no definitive identification of the Westgate Mall terrorists. The nationality and ethnicity of those who casually walked into the Mall on Mwanzi Road, Nairobi on Saturday lunchtime in September of 2013 remains a matter of conjecture. With their AK-47s and packs laden with grenades they set about their indiscriminate (in the beginning at least) slaughter of the innocents, unimpeded before the arrival of various elements of the security services. It remains uncertain as to whether or not they lost their own lives along with those who were cut down by their bullets and bombs. Perhaps some departed along with the groups of hostages who managed to escape. During the four days or so of the siege that followed the initial carnage many did escape and at least one witness claimed to have seen a terrorist amongst them. In such a chaotic situation, it is doubtful we will ever know for certain one way or the other.

It was not the first act of terrorism to be perpetrated in Kenya and it was destined not to be the last but it ranked numerically amongst the deadliest. It was surely one of the most brazen. However, much more than that, the live media coverage meant that to a wide audience the venue could have been their own mall in practically any corner of the globe. It was certain to make many across the world reflect on their own vulnerability, in a similar way to the New York attacks of 9/11 and the London bombings of 7/7. The seeds of insecurity had been sown far and wide.

This has, of course, long been the bedrock of the terrorists' objective, intrinsic to the drive to spread what the term suggests – terror. Terror that has claimed the lives of so many in the name of one deity, cause or another over the centuries.

In the aftermath it was widely accepted that the Kenyan authorities, especially the police and military first responders, were

Prologue

found lacking to say the least. Some soldiers took to looting the shops on an industrial scale even whilst hostages craved rescue. The accusations and counter accusations came quickly but one thing was clear – there was an 'Islamic' element to the aggression. Very soon al-Shabaab stepped up to claim responsibility, purportedly in response to Kenya's decision to send troops into Somalia to help rout them from their strongholds in the south of that country.

In this context the word 'Islamic' is a misnomer. By far the vast majority of those who subscribe to that faith would not recognise the terrorists' behaviour either in Kenya or elsewhere as having any foundation in the religion they follow. There is, however, no disputing the fact that the terrorists went about establishing which amongst the hostages were Muslim and who not. Those who could prove their faith, by either naming the Mother of the Prophet Mohammed or by reciting the Shahada, were released whilst others were murdered.

Various Government Ministers and spokespeople were swift to point out that according to witnesses their attackers seemed to be speaking Somali or Arabic but one of the first reports was more specific, suggesting they were speaking Swahili.

In some ways Kenya can be viewed as two distinct regions: the interior and the coastal region, the latter stretching from the Somali border in the North to Tanzania in the South. This area forms part of the wider 'Swahili Coast' reaching from as far north as Mogadishu and south to Mozambique encompassing Indian Ocean Islands including the Zanzibar and Lamu archipelagos.

Tensions between the Central Government and the predominantly Muslim people of Kenya's Swahili Coast have festered for many years - the secessionist aspirations of the Mombasa Republican Council (MRC) that claims to represent the feelings of the people of the area are well documented. Moreover, many in the Central Government have asserted that the leadership of the MRC is closely linked to that of al-Shabaab, offering their fighters succour, as well as fomenting local empathy with their 'cause' through vociferous preachings inside and out of the Mosques. The claim is that this has resulted in the radicalisation of some amongst the indigenous community. What cannot be denied is that some preachers' rhetoric went far beyond that which could be interpreted as tacit support for al Shabaab. As is so often the case, the lines became blurred. The flames were being fanned with regard to grievances felt by many about the economic neglect of the coastal areas over a long period.

Three clerics in particular were considered, not just by the Kenyan authorities but also by a wider international consensus, to be instrumental in the channelling of so-called Jihadists through Kenya, more specifically Mombasa, to join the ranks of al Shabaab. All three were assassinated in quick succession with the Kenyan Government denying any responsibility. The widespread protests and riots that followed in Mombasa, and to some degree Nairobi, bore witness to the extent of the dissent that the Government feared and allegedly attempted to extinguish with such ultimacy.

Perhaps, therefore, some found it convenient to declare that the Nairobi attackers were speaking Swahili, leaving the distinction between Islamic extremism and social discontent conveniently vague. Along with English, Swahili is a compulsory language taught and spoken throughout the whole of Kenya. But the 'Swahili People' are unmistakeably those from the Swahili coast. Could it have served a political purpose for some to insert the term 'Swahili' into the mix? Was there a veiled suggestion that, although Somalis from Jubaland in the southwest of that country might speak Swahili, or, more accurately, Kiswahili, it was certainly the language of the Kenyans of the coastal areas?

Whatever the case, the Swahili people have proven their sophistication and commercial acumen over many centuries. No matter who has claimed sovereignty over Kenya, the Swahili have always made a positive contribution to the cultural and economic development of the country as a whole. Today's Kenya owes a great deal to the historical part played by the people of the Swahili Coast.

Part One
The Kenya Years

Chapter One

Mombasa Island, approximately 150 square kilometres in area, with its surrounding natural harbour, has been at the heart of East African trade for centuries and by far the greatest influence over the longest period has been that of the Omani Arabs. Throughout history the Omanis, along with the Persians, dominated the trade between Africa on the one hand and the Arabian Peninsular, Persia and India on the other. There is archaeological evidence of this trade dating back to long before the emergence of Islam in the 7th century. However, Islam did take on prominence in the area practically from its conception to the present day, this despite the long periods of custodianship by the Portuguese and later the British.

In the case of the Portuguese throughout the 16th and 17th centuries - and of course the British in the 19th and first half of the 20th centuries - commercial considerations were always going to take precedence over religious, missionary-driven ones. This port was of such strategic significance that accommodations would have to be made. The Portuguese built the enormous fortification still standing today and named 'Fort Jesus'. This became not only their defensive stronghold to which they could retreat but the centre for their lucrative trading interests, most notably the slave trade. Such a defence was necessary not only to repel the advances of other nations who would aspire to occupy this prime spot for their own expansionary trading ambitions, but also those of the local Arabs who would happily have seen the downfall and departure of these colonialists. But it was critical to be able to move freely throughout the area and not just within the walls of their citadel. The only way to do this was to somehow control the region's populace who regularly attacked the fort.

To this end they enlisted the services of the King of Malindi whom they appointed Sultan of Mombasa and who was more than ready to do their bidding in return for the obvious opportunities it afforded him to increase his influence and consequently, his wealth. Underpinned by their Islamic faith and subservience to the Sultan, the acquiescence of those who would otherwise rise-up against them seemed assured. They were now free to go about their exploitation of this jewel on the Indian Ocean coast of Africa, ideally placed to compliment their Indian possession, Goa.

However, a significant amount of local hostility remained and the Arabs eventually laid siege to the fort. The Portuguese called in support from Goa in the form of Indian and Portuguese soldiers, which did relieve but not actually break the siege. After some 33 months the Arabs scaled the walls and in 1698, roughly 200 years after it had begun, the Portuguese reign over Mombasa was brought to an end.

There was ebb and flow to Mombasa's fortunes for some time thereafter – due, in no small part, to rivalry amongst the Omani Arabs themselves. Pressure by the British in the mid 19th century to end the slave trade undoubtedly had an adverse affect on commerce in general. But the subsequent building of the railroad from Mombasa to Uganda reaffirmed the port's prominence in the region.

Even throughout the period of British rule the industrious nature of the Omani Arabs ensured brisk traffic along the traditional trading routes quite apart from those exploited by the colonial power. When a hard fought independence came in 1963 under the leadership of Jomo Kenyatta, Mombasa was thriving on the back of its geographical location.

Throughout the centuries, the consistent influence over the shaping of Mombasa and the rest of the coastal regions and islands has been that of the Swahili people. Occasionally a few would emerge who had the mental agility to assimilate what they saw as the advantageous aspects of western ways, values and education without abandoning or betraying their Islamic faith. In Mjua Kale - Mombasa Old Town – there was indeed such a woman and she was destined to make her diverse ways widely felt beyond the bounds of her immediate Swahili community. Her name was Shamsa Mohammed Muhashamy.

From Within the Stone Walls

Chapter Two

From childhood and throughout her life Shamsa Mohammed Muhashamy was known as Mwana Kutani meaning 'Child from within the Stone Walls', a reference to the old name, Kutani, for the Old Town neighbourhood where her family had lived for generations.

Mwana Kutani entered this world in 1919, the only daughter of five children born to Salim bu Khamisi Muhashamy, a truly enlightened individual. Thanks to his father's sagacity, his uncle's modest wealth and both men's belief in embracing a knowledge of the wider world, Salim had benefited, albeit briefly, from an education in Egypt.

He determined to raise his daughter differently to the way in which the overwhelming majority of girls and young women of her place and time were accustomed. She would be allowed, even encouraged by her father, to join in conversation with visitors to the house or acquaintances on the street. She did sometimes make use of the traditional *Buibui* (veil) and *Leso* (shawl) but her dress was more western than Swahili even wearing a hat and riding a bicycle, quite unheard of in her day. But it is indicative of the pragmatism of her people and society that although they questioned the reasoning behind her father allowing his daughter such freedoms it was more a curiosity than a moral judgement.

She was sent to religious lessons as normal but her father also ensured she had a broader education, something that may well have been afforded the males in her society; he was equally insistent that her "ears and eyes should be similarly opened". He declared that if he were rich he would send them all to Europe for their education.

In her twenties she was militant, mostly in defence of women's rights. She was responsible for small-scale rioting in some cases, although nothing that we would recognise as a riot nowadays. She organised a boycott against the Indian traders' monopoly of the sale of *Leso*, forcing them to sell more fairly for a time. But the resolve of some protesters soon crumbled. She was philosophical about the failure of humans to stick together in support of a cause even when it affected them directly.

She took to improving the organisation of one particular women's dance group known as *Ibinaa*, but this was no ordinary dancing club. *Lelemama* (literally, 'Dance') is an expression of everything feminine in Swahili tradition and in its basic form it would compliment men's dance clubs whilst remaining strictly separate. Fierce rivalry existed between the women's clubs, way beyond normal competitiveness and the slandering by one of another could, and did, lead to open physical clashes; quite often members would need medical treatment for serious cuts and bruises.

Becoming quite obsessive about winning at any cost she broke with all tradition by having her organisation dance 'naked' as she put it, meaning without the Buibui. They also started to dance outside in the streets in full view of men, something unheard of before then: competition had been held in strict privacy with guards posted to stop men seeing the women perform even when they did wear the Buibui.

With maturity, Mwana Kutani saw the folly of her behaviour describing it as 'hooliganism'. She set about reconciling rival groups to form one, more powerful organisation with influence. She had some success but factionalism re-surfaced and she reflected once more on the frailty of the human condition.

From the roots of her upbringing and her later life experiences, a highly intelligent, compassionate woman emerged and one with a strong sense of universal justice. She became a formidable advocate of women's rights, although her social conscience meant that she took up many causes besides. The path to her door was well trodden with people seeking advice and help. She would be asked to assist with everything from obtaining a passport or a birth certificate to acquiring access to the District Commissioner. All, from those who wanted their children to attend school to others who were sick and needed to be hospitalised, would consult her. Mwana Kutani was never known to turn away anyone who asked for her help.

The respect she earned gave her influence in the highest echelons of the machinery of State and she was shrewd enough not to waste it. As election times approached, be they local or national, candidates would be keen to garner her endorsement, thereby ensuring a large proportion of the all-important female vote. Whilst she remained selective in her choice of hopeful, she would not squander the opportunity to elicit some gain from her support - not for herself but for the community as a whole or for an especially deprived section of it.

One of her most impressive achievements was to direct an appeal to Jomo Kenyatta, the first appointed President of the newly founded independent State of Kenya. At a charity event she was called upon to make a speech. With an uncommon confidence she asked the President to commit to making available a piece of land for the purpose of building a school for the Muslim Women's Institute. She was the Treasurer and there was a dearth of such facilities in the neighbourhood at that time. She was a champion of this cause and envisioned facilities for local women to learn English, typing, sewing and other skills.

He immediately agreed to her request and a site was placed at her disposal a few hundred yards south of the Manor Hotel on Mombasa's Nyerere Avenue. Perhaps because it was known that the project had the President's stamp of approval, Mwana Kutani was able to proceed with a little more haste and a little less obstructive officialdom than may otherwise have been the case.

The finished building had a large hall that acted as a community centre as well as a fee-earning venue for seminars, plays and weddings. All of this income added to the coffers of the Women's Institute ensuring that it could continue to empower local women for decades to come.

The courage of one lady with respect and influence to stand up and make her case, when others may have shrunk from the prospect in that revered company, had brought an enormous benefit to a relatively poor community.

Adjacent to the entrance to her house she established a religious school – a Chuoni, the Swahili name for Madrasa. Children from four to eighteen years of age would learn how to read the Koran and be taught the ways of becoming a true Muslim through an understanding of the Five Pillars of Islam.

There would be around twenty children who, having left their footwear by the entrance, would enter to sit on the mkeka - a large woven mat of palm. There were two to cover the floor area. Two teachers would also sit on the mkeka, Bwana Shaishi to take the younger group whilst another would be brought in to teach the older, advanced pupils.

In the evenings the space would be made available for various teachers to give extra tuition to students who may be struggling with any given subject.

None of this work, however, put bread on the table in Mwana Kutani's house. To this end she constructed a large corrugated storage shed to house the wares of her business: she hired out glasses, trays, plates, cutlery and all catering items required for a wedding or a funeral. She enjoyed loyal support from a grateful community.

The tolerance shown by Swahili society, first towards the girl who rebelled so strongly in her early years and then to the woman who conducted her life in such a non-conformist manner, is noteworthy in and of itself. But perhaps more significant is the respect she gained, not just locally within her immediate community but throughout society as a whole.

It would be a common mistake, especially in the West, to assume that a Muslim community would be all-compliant, that any who were not so would be cast out, ostracized or worse. But, for the most part at least, the Swahili people are not so intolerant.

It is true that many had profound reservations about the wisdom, or indeed the reverence of Mwana Kutani's father – similar could be said of her resultant behaviour - but never to the extent that some would imagine.

The vast majority of the Swahili people, especially those from Mombasa and the Kenyan coastal region have, for many years, been more sophisticated than that and they remain so today.

Chapter Three

On April 5th, 1966 in the maternity unit of the Aga Khan Hospital on Vanga Road, a girl was born to 35 year-old Aziza Omar Muhashamy, wife of Masoud Mohammed Muhashamy, some four years her senior. Both born in Kenya, the mother's paternal parentage was Yemeni and her mother was from the Comoros Islands. Masoud's parents were of Omani origin.

The child was not blessed with good health from the start, contracting tuberculosis from which it was doubted she would recover. Malaria followed but fate decreed that she should survive and soon she gained strength along with many precocious talents in her early years. The younger of two sisters, she was named Nur Masoud Mohammed Muhashamy and would be known as Nuru, the Swahili version of the Arabic Nur.

Nuru's sister, Husna, two years older, had been sent to be brought up by their aunt on their father's side but had not settled. Now, at six weeks old, it was Nuru's turn. In both instances it was the aunt who had requested this, partly due to her own inability to have children but it was, in any case, a fairly common practice within the community.

Husna returned to her father to be placed in boarding school near Kitale in Western Kenya where he was District Commissioner. Nuru was to be raised along with two cousins by Mwana Kutani in the house within the stone walls in Mombasa Old Town.

Both parents had been previously married meaning that Nuru was one of a family of stepbrothers and sisters, three girls and four boys on her mother's side and two girls and four boys on her father's. Nuru's mother was her father's second wife, so she immediately had a stepmother as well as her maternal one.

This situation, although common in Swahili society, did not sit well with Masoud's first wife, Rehema, though she was careful not to show her displeasure to her husband. However, if she did accept it with good grace in his presence that was not otherwise the case. The object of her chagrin became the children of his second wife and she employed considerable guile in order to cause them anguish without incurring her husband's wrath. There was little the children could do about this; they knew it and so did Rehema.

Nuru realised very early on that there was genuine love between her father and his first wife and the child would simply not be believed if she raised the matter with him. Besides, he was not easily approachable, despite being very affectionate towards and generally protective of his children.

On the other hand, Nuru's relationship with her aunt was one of complete openness and she eventually confided in her with the result that Mwana Kutani spoke with Rehema on the matter. Rehema bided her time until the opportunity arose to exact a little revenge, which she shrewdly engineered by getting her husband to administer he punishment.

It was so simple: she waited for Nuru and her brother Mohammed, two years her junior, to 'stray', which they inevitably did by staying out a little later than allowed, and she pressed their father to make the children sleep in the yard with Wolfy, the dog. The houseboy eventually took pity on them and let them share a roof for the night but the stepmother had made her point and the children understood it well.

There were many similar instances over the years and as Nuru grew older and bolder Rehema came to understand that she was transparent in front of her stepdaughter. She began to show an exaggerated kindliness towards Nuru when her husband was around. For her part Nuru became more rebellious when he was not. And so the dye was cast between them.

Rehema had other reason to play a pacifying game with Nuru in the presence of the girl's father. During a visit to the house in Kitale, Nuru happened upon her stepmother in bed with her own son. He was in his early twenties. Knowledge of this would be devastating for

Masoud but she had no reason to worry: even at the tender age of eight or nine, Nuru was perfectly aware that her father's pain, should he learn of this, would be unbearable. She loved him far too much to be the bearer of such news.

If Nuru did not consciously make the comparison at the time she clearly understood the manifest contrast between the characters of her stepmother and of her aunt. In many ways history was repeating itself: Nuru's destiny was being shaped by the unconventional upbringing she was receiving in that house in Mombasa just as it had her aunt's before her.

Chapter Four

Everything about being brought up by Mwana Kutani suited Nuru much better than it had her sister. She would be forever grateful for the nurturing she received in that house filled with love and wisdom.

Occasionally, at weekends she would see her siblings, Mohammed, Husna and Salma, on visits to Mombasa with their father.

Nuru has happy memories of these visits but tinged with sadness:

"In the early years, when my Dad visited Mombasa to see my Mum, we would sometimes go for picnics at Bamburi Beach. It was a Public beach. My Mum would prepare sumptuous food and we were like a proper family for a while. My siblings, Husna, Salma, Mohammed and I would splash around in the Indian Ocean and have a laugh with Dad. My Mum would swim with us fully clothed, as is the Muslim code. But she was used to that and she too would have a great deal of fun. We laughed a lot together.
The end of the day was always sad for me because they would drop me off at my aunt's house and the whole of my family would leave together to stay at my Mum's place.
Sometimes I would beg my Dad to convince my Mum to let me stay with her that night and sometimes she would agree. But she would be sure to drop me back at my aunt's first thing the next morning."

On the nights she was dropped off alone, the disappointment tore at Nuru's insides. She had to stand and wave goodbye to her entire immediate family knowing they would be spending the night together close-by at her Mother's house.

But Nuru was a very sensitive, perceptive child. She hid the pain as best she could, figuring that to show it could be hurtful to her aunt. Such internalisation had to have an effect on a child and probably a long term one. Throughout her life she wondered how great a role her feelings of isolation and rejection played in her early adulthood: she always craved love and acceptance.

She may well have been best advised to talk such things through with a professional at some time for when she later tried to do so with her mother, any talk of rejection was dismissed out of hand.

Nuru also loved her trips to visit Kitale during school holidays. Her father would either collect her by car or they would go by bus and train. Either way the whole experience was an exciting departure from her normal life.

On some occasions they would be taken to dinner at the house of her father's English friends, Mr Knight and his wife. After dinner the children would watch as the men played scrabble together. The two of them liked to indulge in a lot of banter about the words proposed by their opponent and Nuru enjoyed seeing her father chuckling and being light-hearted in this way. She was more used to seeing a rather serious and sometimes quite forbidding character.

Her early education was varied. Pre-school was at 'Almeida', run by Goans from India. It was here that she was first taught English. The uniform was immaculate with a kerchief pinned on the left side of the shirt, for blowing your nose or wiping away tears; Nuru came to use it for both.

In keeping with the family's proclivity for ensuring that the children had the advantage of as broad an education as possible, her father applied for a place at Loreto Convent School run by Irish Nuns. Perhaps unusually for a convent school it was co-educational and by necessity the prospectus was secular, respecting the large non-Christian intake. At the age of five this Swahili child was exposed to an entirely different culture and was soon to discern that there was good and bad in all.

Mother Carmel was Mother Superior and she scared the wits out of Nuru and her fellow pupils. A fierce looking woman with freckles, fiery eyes behind horn-rimmed spectacles and tight lips, the children never saw her smile. They were required to curtsy as she passed and she was swift to administer harsh punishment: a rap across the knuckles with a ruler was a regular occurrence for Nuru - spending the remainder of the day in a corner, more so.

But her 'Black Book' was far worse, representing as it did an uncompromising 'three strikes and you're out' policy. By the end of her penultimate year Nuru had managed to accumulate two entries in the book and many of her peers voiced their certainty that she would not survive the final year; she proved them wrong.

If Mother Carmel was the ogress in their lives then Sister Bridget was their deliverance, just as swift to soothe and to offer solace. She was kept busy in that role. Complimenting the good works of Sister Bridget was Nuru's first teacher, Mrs Haig with her loving, caring nature towards her class of 15 or so, each one of whom she seemed able to give individual time and attention. In reporting Nuru's progress she judged her to be 'very shy but determined to learn'.

That's as may be but by the time she was due to be elevated to Standard Seven, Nuru had spent a little too much time performing to the amusement of her classmates and not enough on her studies. As a consequence she was considered to be academically unready and made to repeat her year.

This came as a severe blow, a time filled with disappointment as well as a degree of shame. Her best friends had gone through and one of them, Mahmoud, teased her mercilessly for being 'dumb'.

But it was not all negative. She made new friends who would remain so for years to come and far from being 'dumb' she was bright enough to realise that her teachers were right in their decision: her classroom antics were no longer to feature in her education and she determined to make the best of herself.

From a very early age Nuru was aware that her family did not enjoy the relative wealth of her classmates and she learned not to expose herself to situations where this would become obvious.

On one occasion - she must have been about ten - she was invited to a classmate's birthday party in an upmarket area of Mombasa. The girl was called Afsha Khan and her family's lifestyle was one that Nuru could only dream of.

She approached the house alone and looked through the fence cautiously to assess the situation rather than walking straight in. She was very much aware of her own appearance – dressed in dungarees made of a cheap manmade material – and she suspected her classmates would not be similarly attired; she was right.

On peeking through the fence she saw the girls dressed in smock dresses with ribbons in their hair. The boys were all very smartly dressed too. It was simply too much for her to bear; she was too embarrassed to join them. Instead she decided to kill time walking the street as if she had business to attend to. She didn't want to return straight to her aunt who had dressed her in what she must have thought was appropriate and perfectly fine.

As she walked she decided in her mind that when she had children they would be smartly dressed when they were invited to parties.

On returning home she made up a story about the party in order not to offend her aunt or hurt her feelings. At such a young age she displayed the sensitivities that evade many adults.

From the age of nine, Nuru started performing on stage. Her aunt would organize musical plays under the auspices of the Muslim Women's Institute and Nuru performed Belly Dancing to raise money for the Institute. Her aunt also put together a dance troupe and as a member Nuru performed in front of President Kenyatta at his State House in Mombasa. All the tribes of Kenya performed there. She was talented and kept up her dancing into adulthood.

She already had a deep-seated restiveness within her; a yearning always to discover what was beyond her immediate world. She had listened to her wealthier classmates over the years discussing holidays in Canada, England and elsewhere and she realised the importance of a good education if she was ever to experience such a life for herself.

She was accepted into the Aga Khan School of Mombasa, a co-educational day school. It was her preferred option, given that the only real alternative required her to board. To add to her pleasure her friends Dianna and Vicky were to join her there.

The Aga Khan School was a government establishment, a State School with a much more diverse student base than the three girls had been used to. Their education thus far had included an emphasis on courtesy and etiquette in general. They had been taught to speak English in a very refined manner and now all of this was somewhat out of step with much of the intake at their new school. It was not dissimilar to a Public School pupil in the UK finding themselves in an inner-city academy. They were to get their first real exposure to inverted snobbery – their accent alone was sufficient to give rise to ridicule and a degree of ostracism.

In Nuru's case, all of this was combining with her incomparable home life as well as her genes to subliminally build and strengthen her character and resolve, something she was gradually coming to realise for herself.

Chapter Five

Mwana Kutani was religious, certainly, but not in an intense, fearful way. She would read the Koran and pray five times daily and she ensured that Nuru and her cousins were properly taught the Pillars of Islam, which included sending them to the Madrasa for instruction.

Nuru applied herself to learning the ways and teachings of Islam. She prayed as required, observed Ramadan with its fasting regime and applied the tenets of the religion to her young life as best she could (even if she did swap her curry lunch for a friend's bacon sandwich at times). In common with most religions, all was of course done under the threat of hell and damnation if she didn't. But she was never so cowed by that prospect that she did not question her faith, at least privately.

As is probably the case with most Muslims, she found Ramadan particularly difficult, as intended; whatever else, it is a discipline. But the reward is the festival of Eid al-Fitr.

On the last day of Ramadan her family would ascend the stone and cement stairway to the roof where her aunt had rented out the space to a group of shipyard workers from the Giriama Tribe. They would gather round and try to spot the new moon. One of the Giriama was always the first to see it and they would all hug each other, the children especially excited that from tomorrow there would be no more fasting. They would spend the evening applying henna, which they would sleep in and remove the next morning. It was not acceptable to be adorned with any form of body art in public.

After a breakfast of Mahambri, a kind of donut without the hole, accompanied by peas cooked in coconut milk, they would dress in their new outfits that had been with the seamstress for weeks. Then it was off to knock on the doors of everyone they knew in the neighbourhood to wish them happy Eid. The head of the household would give them some money – a few shillings from acquaintances but a good amount from relatives.

The Kenya Years

For all this, Nuru felt a distance between herself and the rest of the family. They did not share her goals; her lust for the other world she knew was out there. They were content with the prospect of a simple life in their known surroundings with their religious beliefs. She was not at all convinced that Islam or any other religion should dictate one's life. For her, life was in ones own hands to mould and to follow. She vowed to herself that if she had children they would not be raised with any religion. She would teach them respect for others and give them a solid moral foundation on which to build their lives as they chose.

By the time she was 11 years old she was regularly visiting the home of her best friend, Dianna - an entirely different environment to her own - often staying over.

The family would call themselves Christians, although by no means devout or even practising. Dianna was one of three girls and one boy born to a mother from the Kikuyu tribe. Her father was white from the UK. Nuru was welcomed into the house truly as one of the family and she loved Dianna's mother as she would her own, a love she felt was genuinely returned.

The siblings loved to play modern, western music on an old turntable; 'My Boy Lollipop" was a perennial favourite. Their mother used to cook delicious Kikuyu fare for them and Nuru was a regular guest for lunch or dinner.

She saw that, whilst the parents were strict in ways, they also gave the children a great deal more freedom to go out alone and partake in a wide range of activities that would be outside the bounds of normal acceptability for Nuru and her cousins. They would sometimes rent a cottage for the youngsters, supervised by the father, so that they would mix and pass the time freely together, boys and girls, something simply not allowed in Nuru's society. There would be birthday parties held in the evening – surely tantamount to sinfulness - and visits to the Cinema, all as a mixed group.

The parent's were members of the Missions to Seamen Club

over to the West on Moi Avenue near to Kilindini Port where they also ran a simple restaurant. Sometimes they would take the children with them so that they could use the pool, play badminton or use the sports field together. There was also a chapel there where Nuru would join the others for Midnight Mass at Christmas.

The boys were pretty well behaved in the main, although they would have a few beers if the opportunity arose.

Nuru could see no harm in this way of living with its liberal behaviour that was so unacceptable in her Muslim world. More significantly, she perceived a mutual respect here, a more relaxed and voluntary version than the rigid, prescribed one she was used to.

She observed the family celebrating Christmas and they were undoubtedly good people – she was sure they were not on the road to hell even if, according to her Islamic teaching, they were so-called 'non-believers'.

She already craved that someday she would marry a Mzungu (white man) and have a similar loving environment to that which she enjoyed at her friend's house - one where a man showed his wife love and respect. The environment she knew was one where the man always came first and demanded respect regardless of whether he earned it or not.

At her young age, seeing the different lifestyle of her best friend with the English father, she decided she wanted that loving, open family life for herself one day.

Chapter Six

Nuru and her friends became aware of Ahmed Mohammed Hassan within a few weeks of starting at the Aga Khan School for no single reason. He was a good-looking boy for sure, quite shy and well mannered. He did not join in with those who would ridicule the girls for their cultured speech and etiquette but neither did he make any effort to befriend them. There was nothing surprising in this – most young Muslim males of his age could have an aloof edge to them, already aware of their elevated status compared to that of the girls.

Nevertheless, he seemed different somehow; he exuded a quiet confidence. He appeared to have no need to assert his position of gender privilege. Ahmed had a calm about him beyond his years without any hint of arrogance.

They knew little about him other than that he came from a neighbourhood further north on Mombasa Island called Sidiriya; it was not a district any of them would have good reason to visit. There was a large market to the west of Sidiriya called Majengo Market but closer to all their homes was the MacKinnon Market on Nehru Road, a Mombasa landmark since its establishment in 1914.

Close to Ahmed's home in neighbouring Majengo was the renowned Masjid Musa, a large Mosque on Mwabundu Road. People from many districts would travel to join prayers at this famous Mosque but no one from Nuru's family – the men would sometimes attend the Mahdhry Mosque in the Old Town but the females were only likely to do so on their deaths prior to burial.

After school the girls and Ahmed would go their separate ways. Ahmed would take a bus north to his home in Sidiriya, the girls a matatu, or minibus, or sometimes they would cycle. He would return to a home environment very different to Nuru's, but then there were not many quite like hers.

Ahmed's family was no stricter about his religious education than Mwana Kutani was about Nuru's but their outlooks on life were widely divergent. For them the Koran did not just dictate the rules by which they lived, Islam was at the very core of every aspect of their lives. As a consequence, Ahmed grew up with very little latitude in the way he conducted his young life and, unlike Nuru, he had no exposure to the lives of those with other beliefs.

This is not to say that his parents were zealots, simply that they lived as the vast majority did, confident and content to place their religion at the heart of their affairs, guiding their daily thoughts and deeds.

As was normal in his society, apart from his instruction at the Madrasa all his elders mentored Ahmed in the ways of Islam. He led his life as close to his instruction as could reasonably be expected of any young man. It is a fact common to both Ahmed's and Nuru's upbringing that all adults were considered to be responsible for the guidance of all children, not just their own. To this end elders would not hesitate to chastise those who strayed or report them to their family.

In the main, his parents were very tolerant, patiently pointing out the reason he should not err, as they saw it, in this way or that according to the rules of their society, always underpinned by Islam. It was not that he stood out amongst his peers as a particular miscreant or recidivist; on the contrary, he was probably noticed more for his reluctance to go along with the crowd and for the maturity of his demeanour.

He was never quick to engage in acts of physical violence, although he was more than ready to stand his ground if challenged. He did not rush to argument but was articulate enough to defend a passionately held view. He could demonstrate chivalry in the defence of others especially if he judged them weak in the face of intimidation and bullying.

His elders noticed all these qualities and would remark to his parents, often in his presence, that he was 'deep, an old head on young shoulders, an Islamic scholar or cleric of the future perhaps.'

Ahmed did not dwell on such analyses of himself but he did feel somewhat set-apart from most of his friends and classmates, though not at all in the same way that Nuru did. His was more a sense that whatever it was that gave him this feeling of detachment, it would play out within the realms of his known world, not in far off lands of which he had little knowledge and still less interest.

Perhaps they were right to think of him as a future Imam or other Elder but he did not think so. For a start, much of the 'deepness' to which they referred was due to his almost obsessive feeling of unworthiness. He had a consuming doubt in his own faith. He did not believe he was a good Muslim no matter the reassurances of his mentors. He was regularly commended not only for his knowledge of the Koran and the Five Pillars of Islam but on his understanding of the message being imparted by the teachings. But he was not convinced.

So how could his future be within the orbit of Islamic learning and education? He had no wish to pursue his life as a hypocrite – he already felt that way and had no intention of compounding the sin.

There must be something else and despite his self-doubt, his belief in Allah and The Prophet was solid. His life belonged to them and he would wait to see what destiny had in store.

Chapter Seven

The house in Mji Wakale, Mombasa's Old Town, comprised three dwellings. Mwana Kutani and her extended family occupied the main part of the ground floor with the remainder being partitioned off and let to an Indian Muslim family. Men from the Giriama Tribe, all of whom found employment painting ships in the docks, leased the roof space. From time to time these hard working people would return to their villages to visit their families. They would give them the majority of the money they had earned and return to make more. They were a breed of migrant worker who accepted their lot with good grace and they made good neighbours.

The main house consisted of six rooms, three of which formed the area generally used by Nuru and those she would consider her immediate family. She slept on a rolled mattress in her auntie's bedroom. Her aunt shared her bed with her friend, Bi Rukiya whilst Bi Mahfoudha, great aunt to the Sultan of Oman, had a single bed under the window. Outside the window was a small palm tree, which bore the sweetest coconut milk, always offered to any special guest visiting Nuru's aunt.

The living room housed a chiming clock, a brass plate decorated with Arabic writing alongside other brasses and a pair of non-matching sofas. By the front door Mwana Kutani had an armchair where she would sit for most of the morning, reading the Koran and receiving visitors asking for her intervention in the latest problem to beset their lives.

One of Nuru's chores as a child was to polish the brass plates. No branded cleaner from a bottle here, just lemon, dirt and water and a good measure of 'elbow grease' to produce gleaming results.

There was a yellow telephone and, unusually for the neighbourhood, a black and white television set in one corner.

From around 5pm every evening, those who were home would be joined by Nuru's cousins' parents, a few neighbours and, if there was something of particular interest, the people from the Giriama Tribe, to gather round the set.

At news time, silence was required from all; Bi Mahfoudha would be quickly angered if anyone – usually one of the children - interrupted the news. If it continued, without a word she would walk over to the TV and simply turn it off. This naturally annoyed the assembled company immensely but such was the respect commanded by her, mainly due to her bloodline, that her actions were accepted without question. The children soon learned not to make a murmur once the news came on.

The third room was simply partitioned with hardboard to make a bedroom used by Bi Rukiya's son, the thirty-something year old Ahmadi. A very quiet, private individual, he would leave early in the morning to work at the docks returning around 7.30 in the evening to lock himself in his room. Later in life he relocated leaving little impact on the lives of those he left behind.

The room also contained a locked wardrobe wherein Mwana Kutani kept some of her clothes as well as some of Nuru's. There were also a few valuables and a machine with a stethoscope that cousin Khuleta used for monitoring her aunt's blood pressure. Later, Nuru would take over the task with equal competence.

Opposite the door to Ahmadi's room stood a refrigerator and a locked dry-foods cupboard, to be opened only by Mwana Kutani and her two friends: there were too many people living in the combined accommodations, as well as many other comings and goings, to allow general access.

To the right of the door, the crudely finished stone and concrete stairs led to the roof space where the Giriama lived and where the cook would prepare lunch for those living below. Nuru's aunt would measure by cup the rice required for the number lunching that day, normally to be accompanied by a curry of fish or chicken.

The open part of the roof space also served as a communal drying area for the laundry that would be laid flat and secured at the corners with stones.

To one end of the main ground floor living space was a dining area with a table to seat eight*. Nuru always sat next to her aunt who was at the head of the table. Opposite Nuru sat a recurrent presence at lunch and one that did not enhance the children's enjoyment of it.

Fatuma Ali had an open lunch invitation from Mwana Kutani that she chose to take up on a daily basis. To the children she was a harridan with a negative outlook on life, always ready to scold them for the slightest misdemeanour – or no misdemeanour at all. They all agreed that she was a lot nicer to the neighbourhood cats than she was to them. She had an exceptionally dark complexion that she exaggerated with black eyeliner called Wanda and the whole forbidding package was topped off with an all-pervading odour of sour milk.

Nuru could feel the cruel eyes of this harpy-like individual on her as she ate, waiting for her to err in some small way, and it made

The Kenya Years

her flesh crawl - a feeling that failed to abate over the many years of these lunchtime gatherings.

Near the dining table was an old chair where the cook, Mwana Idd, would sit waiting to be told what she should prepare for lunch, the only meal regularly taken together as a family.

A few feet away from the main table was a tap and basin on a raised step that was used for everything from washing dishes to cleaning fish. If the Giriama people wished to buy water for a few shillings, they would be allowed to fill a bucket there.

It was here that Nuru would sit at weekends from the age of about ten to grate coconut. The method used is similar in many parts of the world but in Mombasa the special stool is known as Mbuzi. It narrows towards the front to house a sharp, grooved blade and the seated person would take a half coconut with both hands and grate the inside clean. Afterwards, the grated coconut would be placed in a pouch made from woven palm frond that was then squeezed and wrung to produce the first batch of condensed coconut milk. This was put to one side. Next, water would be added to the mulch and the pouch squeezed again until there was no more milk to be had. The remains were thrown for the birds.

Next to the step a door led to another living room with bedroom beyond, once occupied by Mwana Kutani. Latterly she had vacated it to provide living quarters for her nephew, Mohammed, his wife - also named Rukiya - and, eventually, their six children. Rukiya had a sewing machine and worked as a seamstress, always with a large backlog of jobs that she never seemed to get on top of. He worked as a driver for tourists at a game lodge, returning to regale Nuru and the others with exaggerated tales of his adventures in the bush. He was a slightly naïve man always building castles in the air, which he was destined never to realise due mainly to the fact that he and his family lived a hand to mouth existence. In any event, he died at a young age of diabetic complications, dreams unfulfilled.

Adjacent to the door to their room there was a big concrete seat where Nuru and her cousins and friends – sometimes just her imaginary friend – would play whilst others were enjoying a siesta. Occasionally someone would be cooking on the stove that sat there and there was also a large square table where they would do their ironing. The children were expected to iron their own school uniforms by the time they were nine or ten and this could be quite a challenge. The iron had to be filled with hot coals and everyone prayed they did not burn their clothes.

Opposite the stove a wooden door led to the toilet, shower and tap that everyone used except for the Indian neighbours and the Giriamas. The toilet was partitioned but still open to one side and it was of the Arabic squatting style with the tap and shower to the side. It was advisable to spend as little time as possible in there so one would take in toothpaste and soap to ensure that ablutions were completed in one visit. And if you were unfortunate enough to have to follow someone else then it had better be one of Nuru's cousins, Mohammed or Khuleta (who Nuru always called 'Big Sister'): from their mid-teens onwards, both smoked which helped mask the stench.

Returning to the front of the house, large concrete steps led down from the front door to a corrugated iron gate to the street. To the right of the door there was a concrete seat where Nuru and her cousins and close neighbourhood friends would hang out in the evenings next to the fragrant Yasmini bush. There were a few more plants around but no grass, just earth, and this was their garden.

To the right of the last step sat the small building that Mwana Kutani had built to house her Chuoni – the school for children to learn their Koran and the ways of Islam.

Towards the back of the house a door led to a small room with a bed that for some years was occupied by Azzad, another son of Bi Rukiya. A single man in his thirties, he was highly intellectual having enjoyed the benefits of a good education. He was not religious in the sense that he would pray as ordained by Islam and he did not attend the Mosque. But he did pray openly from time to time and, in light of his behaviour towards her, it was this that led Nuru to brand him a hypocrite, albeit only to herself.

As time had gone by, Bi Rukiya and Bi Mahfoudha had taken to eating at a small table set for them in the living room – somewhat elitist one might say. To understand why the great aunt of the Sultan of Oman should be living here at all requires some historical context:

> The Archipelago of Zanzibar had long been a protectorate of the United Kingdom, classified as a Sultanate. The UK did not claim to be any more than its Protector although it had earlier used military force to install a Sultan deemed favourable to its interests. Up to the death of SAID bin Sultan in the 1850s Zanzibar had been part of the Sultanate of Oman and Zanzibar. The Sultan even chose to move his residence from Muscat to Stone Town on the main Island of Unguja, widely known simply as Zanzibar. In 1963, however, the UK decided that Zanzibar should become an independent, self-governing State within the Commonwealth. That status lasted for less than a month and in January 1964 left wing-cum-communist factions of African ethnicity combined to take control in the Zanzibar Revolution. Sultan Jamshid bin Abdullah, (aka Sayyid Sir Jamshid bin Abdullah Al SAID) was forced to flee to London with his entourage and ministers. The newly self proclaimed State of the Peoples' Republic of Zanzibar and Pemba lasted until the April when it was united with Tanganyika – undoubtedly the instigators of the revolt - to become the United Republic of Tanganyika and Zanzibar.
>
> Bloody retribution for the years of inequality followed with many Arabs and South Asians being slaughtered. Those who could flee did and Bi Mahfoudha, who had

indeed enjoyed the privileges of the ruling elite, escaped to Mombasa. There she was directed to the house of Mwana Kutani who would surely guide and help her in her plight.

In 1970 Bi Mahfoudha's great nephew, Qaboos bin Said al Said overthrew his father in a palace coup to become Sultan of Oman. Overnight Bi Mahfoudha had become a member of the ruling Omani Royal Family, affording her a degree of financial security. She had acquired a weekend flat for herself where she installed a cook who delivered meals to her in Kutani - delicious smelling fare that left the children curious and a little jealous. She now chose to enjoy this at the separate table with Bi Rukiya.

She had not arrived from Zanzibar penniless and it was thanks to her that the house had the rare distinction, in that district at least, of owning a telephone and television – a television that she felt perfectly entitled to turn off as she pleased, regardless of the feelings of others. The financial improvement associated with her newly elevated status meant that the household would also be the first to swap the black and white set for the new colour version.

And the telephone meant that she could and did receive regular, perhaps weekly, calls from her son in Oman – now very much a member of the inner circle. But she had no desire to live elsewhere on a permanent basis.

Parcels would sometimes arrive from Oman with various gifts, elaborate garments and delicacies but one such package left them all wondering for some days: On opening it Bi Mahfoudha found a jar filled with water. They puzzled what could be so special about this water from Oman – had they been Catholic they may have suspected it had been blessed but there was nothing similar in Islam. And even if Oman did have beautiful spring water from the mountains it was not something that people generally took to bottling and mailing to friends and relatives. The following weekend her son telephoned and after the usual pleasantries asked her if she liked the watch he had sent her to which she replied, 'Watch?'... 'Yes' came the reply from her son, 'I sent you a Rolex Oyster; didn't you think it was a great idea of mine to put it in a jar of water to show you that it was water proof?'

Somewhere between Oman and Mombasa someone was considerably richer that day than their wages would have made them. They all knew that the watch would never be recovered.

Chapter Eight

Nuru was a pretty young girl and at an early age looked mature beyond her years. It was not that she enhanced her appearance by the use of cosmetics and it was not that she was allowed to dress beyond her years. Nonetheless, at nine years of age she was approaching puberty and already had a natural awareness of her own development and the first stirrings within her of youthful womanhood. What she did not have - what she could not have at this early age - was a definitive sense of her own prerogative to decide what was and was not proper about an adult's behaviour towards her - nor should there be any expectation that she should. Her friendships and social activities outside the house were monitored not only by her aunt but also by Swahili society as a whole. This was neither the age nor the place for formal sexual education but rather an environment where her female elders would judge the timing for, and level of, the information deemed necessary as transition from adolescence to puberty dictated.

Azzad was aware that the child was fond of him and rather than recognise her innocence, chose to place his own wholly inappropriate interpretation on that fondness and to take advantage of it. The limit of his wrongdoing did not go beyond kissing and fondling but the intimacy was quite invasive and of course completely deplorable. At the time, Nuru was in no way equipped to realise or to understand the seriousness of his unseemly transgressions.

The way in which she dealt with this episode serves to demonstrate the substance of Nuru; the character instilled in her by nature – her genes, and by nurture – the upbringing by her aunt.

She neither bore any guilt nor did she feel a victim; she had no wish to carry with her either of those burdens. As she became more aware of the wider world she certainly realised that incidents no more serious often resulted in the course of a young life being altered forever and not for the better. Many abused would go on to abuse others, arguably through no fault of their own but as a direct result of the initial violation thereby creating an insidious, self-perpetuating cycle of misery.

Once she was old enough to realise the unacceptability of Azzad's behaviour and still later to be capable of rationalising it, she was able to reflect on the incidents, for there was more than one, with stoicism and a sense that it was done and could not be changed. She would extract from the experience whatever positives she could and take forward yet another lesson on her fellow man.

Thankfully for Nuru she became philosophical about the whole sordid business, accepting the fact that we will all fail many tests of probity throughout our lives and she was intelligent and humble enough to include herself in that certainty. She was content not to stand in judgement over one man's weakness any more than she wished to be judged herself, either then or in the future.

Unfortunately, she later became aware that similar abuse occurred elsewhere within the extended family (and, she suspects, does so to this day) making it more difficult to sustain a pragmatic, forgiving attitude towards her own. Many abused carry a futile sense of guilt that their own inaction may have contributed to the abuse of others, no matter how extreme the disconnect between the individual instances. But the key word here is 'futile'.

She encountered more incidents of abuse in her early teens and realised that this was not something entirely confined to her own Swahili community. An irregular afternoon or evening visit was to the house of a school friend with a white, European father whose precise nationality she did not commit to memory. On one such occasion, which prompted a tapering off of further visits, the father chose a moment when Nuru was on her own to call her into the bedroom where he promptly placed her hand on his erect penis. With his wife and others in the house at the time, he obviously intended to go no further and so it was an act of arrogance as much as one of depravity and he enjoyed Nuru's discomfort.

As far as Swahili society is concerned it seemed to her that although there was an awareness that abuses were taking place, there was a distinct absence of any willingness to confront the perpetrators. Perhaps there is little difference in the way in which Swahili society dealt with – or failed to deal with - the sexual abuse in their midst compared to Western society at that time. When identified, suspects might be shunned and people did talk guardedly about certain individuals being 'cursed' because of their molesting ways.

But an individual being 'cursed' raises an interesting concept, seemingly at odds with the Islamic beliefs of the Swahili. Alongside their adherence to Islam, the Swahili maintained what could best be described as spiritual beliefs, albeit not openly. It would be natural for an outsider to attribute this to the Bantu element of their heritage but in practise, activities in pursuit of those beliefs were verbalised in Arabic rather than Swahili. These beliefs probably have their origins in the essence of what it means to be Swahili – the historic mixing of Bantu and Arabic blood.

Nuru knew that one of the teachers (a Mwalimu in Swahili or Maalim in Arabic) in Mwana Kutani's Chuoni had been the subject of just such a curse: he had a dressing over an open wound on one finger that simply would not heal whatever the treatment. It was widely known that he molested children – Nuru never asked her aunt why he was tolerated at the Chuoni - and no one was in any doubt that this was how he had been marked as the result of 'Kurogwa'.

'Kurogwa' is the Swahili word for 'curse' or 'cursed' or perhaps more accurately, 'deserved consequences' – loosely speaking similar to 'hassad' in Arabic or the Hindu or Buddhist 'Karma'. It is an extension of their faith, an adjunct to it rather than witchcraft, and was widely practised, if not openly talked about. Nuru witnessed Mwana Kutani herself summoning such a 'Kurogwa' on one occasion. On opening the gate to the street one morning they discovered that someone had defecated on the doorstep. Mwana Kutani could not think of a reason for this or who may be responsible for the fetid pile but neither did she care about identifying him – they were sure it must be a 'him'. She gathered some hot coals and ash that she poured onto the faeces whilst muttering a few words in Arabic. On being questioned by Nuru she did not tell her the nature or translation of her Arabic murmurings but she said that they would soon know the culprit because he would start scratching his arse and not be able to stop. And so it transpired.

It would not be fair to characterise these beliefs as superstitions belonging to African tribal lore for they were clearly aligned with the Swahili's Islamic faith. At times prayer would be related to giving thanks but it could also be used for protection from jealousy or envy. If something had been lost, Mwana Kutani would say a dua – a prayer – from the Koran and Nuru recalls its effectiveness on more than one occasion but one in particular. When she was probably nine years old, she had been fighting with a girl in the town who had managed to pull off one of her gold hoop earrings. She looked for it afterwards but simply could not find it. Her aunt said a dua and told her to return to the place and look again. On her return the earring was in plain view - quite bizarre.

There would be a dua for travelling too. If Nuru visited her father, her aunt would take her hand and move it as though she was drawing a picture on the wall whilst calmly reciting the appropriate dua. Nuru took great comfort from it.

Chapter Nine

It was Thursday afternoon and school had finished for the week. Ahmed looked forward to this third weekend of the month with relish; he would be spending time with his cousin Ali at his house across the Nyali Bridge in Kisauni. Ali's father owned a large haulage business, trucking goods up-country and into Tanzania and Uganda from Mombasa Port. He also owned a fleet of dumper-trucks operating in the construction industry and the whole concern had proven very lucrative over the years.

The boys' fathers were ill at ease in each others company but on most Fridays together they would attend the Masjid Musa close to Ahmed's home.

To Ahmed's father's vexation, Friday prayers, or at least the Imam's rhetoric following them, would sometimes prove to be the catalyst for a demonstration against one thing or another. The two fathers, although brothers, held diametrically opposed views about showing dissent, even when they agreed on the subject matter.

Ahmed's father preferred the quieter, patient-but-steadfast approach. He was not at all comfortable with the way in which his brother was all too ready to join in with the mob's railing against the government and anyone else they had been told had done them a misdeed. Worse than this, he encouraged his son, Ali, to join him, which quite naturally he did. Ahmed, even without his own father's forbiddance, did not.

Regardless of this marked difference between the families, Ahmed's father deemed his brother to be a good man at heart. He considered him to be basically respectable, despite his occasional Friday afternoon digressions. Consequently, he agreed that his son be allowed to spend some time with his cousin at their house across Tudor Creek.

Ali was the eldest of four boys and the family lived in much finer surroundings than Ahmed was used to back in Sidiriya. He had access to the latest TV and Audio technology as well as devices for playing the new TV games. It was all quite amazing to Ahmed but Ali took it pretty much for granted. He would quickly tire of it all after arriving home with his cousin. In any event, much more than his cousin, Ali enjoyed considerable freedom to roam and Ahmed was happy to join him and his friends in the surrounding streets and alleyways. They played impromptu games of soccer, chatting and looking for opportunities to indulge in anything that would be frowned upon by their elders.

On these weekends, Ahmed did go along with the crowd and he thoroughly enjoyed indulging his youthful rebelliousness as much as any of them.

For all this, he could not find any empathy with Ali or his father when it came to their Friday afternoon antics, especially as they invariably had overtones of religious bigotry. He had no time for the ranting of the Imam following prayers. This was simply not the way Ahmed and his family interpreted Islam and it was certainly not the way they incorporated its teachings into their daily lives.

In his neighbourhood on the Island there were plenty who joined in with the Friday fracas but here in Kisauni such people seemed to be in a majority. It was the only reservation he held about going there.

It all seemed incongruous to Ahmed: Ali and his family did not seem to lead their daily lives like devout Muslims and yet they acted upon the words of the Imams like true devotees. He could not understand how they reconciled this anomaly.

In his early teens Ahmed did not have the temerity to vocalise these observations or to seek a better understanding; in later years he was not so reluctant.

Chapter Ten

Measured against any expectation of what may be considered a fair and equitable marital contract, it would be difficult not to judge Nuru's father harshly. But that may simply be a Western perspective.

Masoud had taken two wives as was his Islamic right, but neither lived with him on a permanent basis. Whilst he lived in a good degree of luxury in Kitale - where he was afforded the privileges associated with his position as District Commissioner - he preferred to keep his wives in relative penury some 900 kilometres distant in Mombasa.

Whilst married to Rehema he had started an affair with Aziza, herself married to a butcher called Ahmed. By 1961 they had conceived a baby, Zahra, born the following year. Zahra was to be brought up by a distant cousin of Aziza's and for many years the situation was not discussed within the family. Later, Zahra would sometimes join Nuru and her siblings on trips to visit their father and their resemblance to each other could hardly have been lost on anyone. But it was not openly acknowledged. Masoud did provide some help for the upbringing of the child but not as openly as he did for Nuru.

By 1963 Masoud had persuaded Rehema to accept Aziza as his second wife and they were duly married, producing their second child, Husna in 1964.

At his behest Rehema would spend some months with him. Nuru's mother would join him for 2 weeks at the most during school holidays in July or at Easter time. In the absence of his two wives, Masoud did not lead a life of celibacy and his children were well aware of the existence of his girlfriend, Hanna, a sophisticated, well educated lady from the Kikuyu people.

Sometimes Hanna would phone to speak to him during Aziza's visits and he would speak to her in English knowing that Aziza would not be able to understand. But she understood enough to ask the children for a translation after he had left the room, placing them in an invidious position. None of them wished to get involved in their parents' arguments, which were not confined purely to the matter of his affair: occasionally his attitude towards her could be quite severe. But the other side of the coin was that she would nag and badger him relentlessly at times. So they all learned to avoid giving Aziza the true translation.

Masoud was 'careful' with his money, but he gave both wives an allowance sufficient to keep each of them in modest accommodation. They could afford decent food, good clothing and a houseboy or girl but they would never have the loving, sharing relationship for which both of them yearned.

Aziza was a very beautiful woman who loved the finer things in life and, mostly thanks to the considerable support of her favourite son, Omar, she was able to wear fashionable clothes and to travel a little.

She was fortunate to visit Omar in Dubai where he lived from the age of 20. Friends invited her to visit them in Dallas where their generosity ensured she had a real taste of the good life for a while. She managed to go on the Hajj to Mecca and made several trips to London. She may have gone to Oman on one occasion but little is known of that visit. In Mombasa, for the most part, she did her utmost to lead as flamboyant a lifestyle as funds allowed, 'gallivanting with her friends', as both her and her husband's families liked to call it. But always without the loving companionship she craved.

Masoud had provided Aziza with a flat on Vanga Road opposite the Aga Khan Hospital close to Nuru's High School. This would be about 20 minutes drive south from the flat he had made available to Rehema but the two wives were not in the habit of meeting. On occasions Nuru would visit her mother for lunch. Sometimes, not often, she would stay overnight, but she was aware of the additional pressure this placed on her mother: because Aziza shared the flat with her eldest daughter, Warda, space was at a premium.

It was a two-bedroom flat with a small kitchen, one bathroom, a shower and one toilet. It had small balconies to the front and rear ideally situated for one of the family's favourite pastimes: people-watching. They would spend hours making up fictitious lives and occupations for the passers-by below.

Into this small space squeezed Aziza, Warda and her three children as well as Nuru's siblings who may be visiting. This meant that at times there would be six staying even before Nuru's arrival. (In later years, Warda was married and then widowed leaving her with her three children and three stepchildren to bring up with Aziza's help in that small flat).

For this reason Nuru always felt that she was an additional burden on her mother. Even so, Aziza would be sure to wake early in order to make one meal for everyone before going off 'gallivanting' with her friends. After that they would all fend for themselves - always available: eggs, toast or the Swahili donut with milk.

Nuru was often very quiet in the company of others, a product, perhaps, of her sense that she belonged to another time and place. At the time it seemed no more than an improbable dream, a yearning for a world beyond hers. But she was not always withdrawn during her visits; years later she held happy memories of those times too, memories of fun with her siblings swapping silly stories and not minding the overcrowded conditions at all.

She saw that her mother was different in so many ways to Mwana Kutani, now showing some kindness towards others, now mean in spirit. She never treated Nuru in the same way as Husna or Mohammed. During the most crowded times she would sometimes allow them to share her large bed but never Nuru – she was always made to sleep on a rug on the floor...even when nobody else was sharing her mother's bed. (Mwana Kutani, on hearing of this, bought her a roll-up mattress to keep at her mother's flat to at least make the floor a little more comfortable.) This apparent distinction between her feelings for Nuru and her siblings, further added fuel to Nuru's sense of isolation within the family.

On one occasion she visited at the same time as her sister and brother were staying only to find them and their mother packing to visit their father. Nuru's mother told her that she did not have the money to take her along with them to which Nuru replied that she would run home and ask her aunt for the fare. Her mother agreed saying that they would be leaving the next day. The following morning Nuru returned with her fare and her small bag to find that they had all left earlier. No note, no explanation - and no love, thought Nuru. It would not be the last time that she would experience her mother's cruelty and bad faith.

Aziza could be unnecessarily unpleasant towards the houseboy or girl too. Sometimes she would lock the poor unfortunate in the house whilst she went on her errands to make sure he or she didn't leave until the house was spotless and their chores completed to her satisfaction. Nuru was aware that she often drew comparisons between her mother and her aunt whose approach to life and to people seemed so at odds. But she also saw that her mother could be kind at times and wondered which of her dispositions was the true reflection of the person inside.

She understood the frustrations her mother must have - she was trapped in a lifestyle she would not choose for herself. At the same time she had glimpses into the world she would prefer with little or no prospect of ever reaching that distant star. Her lack of a decent education meant that she could not support her preferred way of life by working and so she was destined by circumstance to take her pleasures whenever the opportunities presented themselves.

In analysing her mother's situation in those early years Nuru's aspirations intensified. To her mind it was clear that broader-minded, mutually loving relationships did exist...but they did so outside of traditional Swahili society.

By the time she reached her mid-teens Nuru was spending more and more time with families of mixed European / Kenyan parentage, invariably of Christian faith, especially the family of her close friend

Dianna Naylor. Their house was of concrete construction with a thatched roof and they had a small cottage in the grounds where Dianna's brother Paul lived. He was the second child of four: Jean, the eldest, Paul the only boy then Dianna and her younger sister Suzie. There were three bedrooms in the main house, a master for the parents, Jean in the second and Dianna and Suzie in single beds in the third. All beds were fitted with Mosquito nets due to the infestation in the southern part of Mombasa Island where they lived. A cosy patio with a comfortable old sofa was a favourite place for the children to hang out after school.

Neither Mwana Kutani nor anyone else in Nuru's household would have approved of the Naylor's way of life; they certainly would not have condoned Nuru's participation in it. By now the schism between her way of thinking and that of her family, or indeed of the Islamic aspect of Swahili society as a whole, was pretty much entrenched. Out of deference to her aunt, she tried not to flaunt her disillusionment with religion at home but she did not respect her family's faith. She had no wish to argue for her beliefs over theirs but she knew what she wanted for herself.

The dilemma she faced was how to lead the life she preferred without causing unnecessary anguish to her aunt and the only solution was an age-old one: she lied about it.

Having told her aunt that she was going to spend the weekend with her mother – aunt and mother did not communicate regularly – she would in fact stay with Dianna and her family. Dianna's parents were very accommodating and would allow the teenagers a great deal of freedom going so far as to take them to a party if there was one, collecting them again at midnight; this would not have been an option for Nuru had her aunt known about it.

In 1983, at almost seventeen, Nuru finished her High School with grades that left her with limited options. She decided that she would follow some other members of the family who had found themselves in a similar position and enrol in hairdressing school

The Kenya Years

in Nairobi. Nuru's aunt was patently not a stupid woman. She was well aware that Nuru was straying from the path she should follow according to the family's faith and traditions. In any event, quite apart from the disappointing grades, the situation had reached the point where an ultimatum was about to be put before the 'wayward one'.

Mwana Kutani sat Nuru down and, in the presence of 'big sister' Khuleta, told her that she would now live with her father who had since moved to the capital. She must behave herself there or she would be taken out of the hairdressing school and married to her second cousin, several years her senior.

Such a marriage, Nuru knew, would result in a life somewhat different to the one she planned for herself. She would be absolutely forbidden to pursue any outside interests. The highlights would be attending Muslim weddings, cooking and raising as many children as her husband pleased. Swahili society may have tolerated liberal minded people like her aunt – perhaps a singular exception – but marriage generally followed the traditional Muslim design. Nuru readily accepted her aunt's conditions.

Under the threat of a Muslim marriage to a remote cousin, she travelled to Nairobi to learn her profession and lead her life under the watchful eye of her father. Given her loftier ambitions to marry a Mzungu, lead a westerner's lifestyle and travel the world, surely she would ameliorate her ways to avoid such an unpalatable alternative? Surely?

Chapter Eleven

A few years earlier, Masoud Mohammed Muhashamy had accepted a position as Deputy Permanent Secretary in local government in Nairobi. He also took up the Chairmanship of the Kenya Shipping Agency located in Mombasa. His home and immediate surroundings in Kitale had been more than acceptable but his new Nairobi residence was much more sumptuous in a smart, gated community housing Embassy officials, mostly Norwegian. There were several such estates in a district called Westlands.

There were perhaps 30 detached homes set in an oval in extensive grounds that included a children's play area with swings, slides and roundabouts. In her early teens Nuru, her siblings and cousins had discovered that you could tour almost the entire estate by way of the rooftops, jumping one to the other - father would not have approved! Nuru had good memories of her times there shared with her siblings. Masoud lived there for two to three years before moving to another similar estate in the Langata district of Nairobi, which is where Nuru joined him in 1983.

This was the first opportunity for Nuru to really get to know her father. She lived there with her two siblings and he found three teenagers living under the same roof a considerable challenge. His answer was to lay down strict rules about the way they should conduct themselves, most especially the hours and company they kept. And he kept a very close eye on their compliance, or, in Nuru's case, non-compliance. He would sometimes take himself off for long weekends with his girlfriend, Lydia, leaving the teenagers with just the houseboy. Masoud's relationship with Hanna had ended with his departure from Kitale; Lydia was his secretary, who later became his third wife and bore him three children.

The youngsters didn't mind him taking weekends away as they could invite their friends over without being subjected to his constant scrutiny. This was a time when Nuru could at last bond with her siblings and even though Husna was only home in the holidays they shared a bedroom and drew closer together. But where Nuru was concerned, living with her father was never going to end well.

Nuru had a friend on a neighbouring estate, Lorna, who she liked to go clubbing with. Her father would never have sanctioned this so Nuru would wait until he had gone to bed, lock her door and climb through the window to wait by the gate to the entrance to the estate for her friend to pick her up. Lorna's boyfriend had a car and either he or his brother would drive them. Nuru would wait for the hoot, climb over the gate and together they would head off for Nairobi's vibrant club scene. She would ensure that she returned by the same route before her father rose in the morning. But Nuru was always bound to push her luck.

She had a natural flair for hairdressing and was becoming quite accomplished at it. She started to receive requests from neighbours and she could make a fair bit of money after college and at the weekends. Her father even had enough confidence in her skills to ask her to do Lydia's hair, which was flattering and naturally she agreed. He did not, however, say when this should be and Nuru thought no more of it.

It was Friday night, Masoud had left to visit his girlfriend and Nuru had clubbing in mind. She met up with Lorna and the two boys in the usual way – just because her father was not there did not mean she should compromise the houseboy's position. She locked her door from the inside and made her normal, clandestine rendezvous with her friends. In the early hours Lorna persuaded Nuru to stay with her for the night and return home in the morning; and whyever not? What could possibly go wrong?

Unknown to Nuru, her father had decided that this particular Saturday would be the day for Nuru to do Lydia's hair. He returned home late on the Friday night with a view to taking Nuru over to his girlfriend's home the next day. On his return he did not knock on her door, assuming she would be sleeping at that hour. The next morning, however, he did knock and of course received no reply. He fetched a spare key and entered to find a bed that had not been slept in. He was probably not entirely surprised and immediately drew the correct conclusion. Rushing to find his son, he demanded to know where his sister was but Mohammed genuinely did not know.

Masoud told his son that he was extremely angry and disappointed in his sister and to tell her on her return to pack her belongings and leave his house; He did not want to see her on his return.

Nuru was about to enter a whole new world, far removed from the luxury and security she had become used to at her father's house in the gated community in the upmarket district of Langata.

Chapter Twelve

Nairobi in the early 1980s was a capital city bursting with vitality, arguably more than any other in the whole of sub-Saharan Africa.

The city was alive with the optimism of independence, despite the passing of Kenya's founding father and most revered President, Jomo Kenyatta in 1978. Daniel Arap Moi now held the reigns, claiming to walk in his predecessor's footsteps, an assertion that was widely accepted in the early years. A bungled 1982 coup attempt by two ill-coordinated factions - students on the one hand and junior ranks from the Air Force on the other - gave him further ammunition to set about tribal cleansing of the government. The Kikuyu bore the main brunt of his despotic aspirations. However, he was an extremely capable politician managing to hold on to power for 24 years despite a litany of allegations of human rights abuses and corruption throughout much of that time.

For the vast majority of Nairobi's residents, none of this was of foremost importance in their daily lives. But there were Kenyans with a keen interest in their country's politics and future direction including those who were overtly opposed to Moi's one-party rule. One way or another such dissent was invariably quashed or nullified.

A case in point is that of the freelance journalist, Mary Anne Fitzgerald who had been a thorn in Moi's side for some time. She recalled how she was awoken in the early hours by Moi's secret police, given two hours to pack essentials and summarily deported. South African born Fitzgerald had lived in Kenya with her family, which included an adopted Samburu boy, for 22 years, and spoke fluent Swahili. None of this held any sway in Moi's Kenya.

But at street level Nairobi throbbed with the daily urgency of breadwinning and the nightly beat of a club-scene second to none on the continent.

Having been greeted by her brother with the news that her father did not wish to see her in his house on his return, Nuru was taking the 15-minute walk to Lorna's house. Her options were limited: return to her aunt's house in Mombasa to be promptly married off to her cousin or...well, what? She needed at least a breathing space to figure out her next move and she hoped that Lorna and her parents would provide it.

Lorna's parents were Seychellois. Her mother had light skin and to Nuru, a mystifying accent when she spoke English. Her father was darker with a similar accent but one that Nuru somehow expected in his case. Nuru told her friend the situation and asked to stay for a few days. Lorna asked her parents but decided to finish the explanation at 'a few days' without elaborating on the reasons why. They agreed.

Nuru had no plan at this stage but there was no future in this subterfuge. Once the mother started to ask when Nuru would be returning home she decided she must come clean and asked to stay on a longer basis. In return she would help around the house with cooking and cleaning in addition to keeping up her hairdressing training. She could also pay her way as hairdressing was now giving her a reasonably steady income. They agreed to this arrangement and to Nuru's relief allowed her to stay.

Lorna had two younger brothers of around 14 and 8 years old so Nuru would sleep in Lorna's room, which suited them both. They had become close friends and as teenagers they bonded like sisters, very much enjoying their time together. But Nuru was well aware that this situation could not persist indefinitely: she was in transit without having the first clue as to her next destination.

She didn't mind cooking for the family and perhaps making up lunch for the younger brother, Kit, from time to time. The family made her feel very welcome. Lorna's mother put on a façade of strictness sometimes but she also displayed a wicked, sardonic sense of humour whilst being very caring for her family. Although very much the man of the house, her father was a witty, light-hearted and fair-minded individual. Together, the parents created a liberal, loving environment that made Nuru feel very comfortable, much the same as she had in Dianna's home in Mombasa.

They were quite relaxed about allowing Lorna and Nuru to enjoy their teenage years and this included Friday nights clubbing, although they did expect them to return home at a 'reasonable hour'. The girls respected this despite Nuru not being prepared to do so during her time at her father's house.

'Carnivore' has long been an internationally acclaimed restaurant on Langata Road in the south of Nairobi. Over many years its annexe, the Simba Saloon, has hosted some of the best-known exponents of African and African-influenced music as well as giving its revellers the latest offerings from the western music scene.

Locals just called the whole place 'Carnivore' in all its incarnations and this was the weekend destination of choice for a wide spectrum of Nairobi society. From the less well off who managed to scrape enough together to shed their yokes once in a while, to the wider indigenous society. From the wealthy children of the expat community to the well-heeled members of the diplomatic corps, Carnivore was THE place to go.

In the mix would be the odd 'Lady of the Night' plying her trade as well as the usual smattering of undesirables looking for an opportunity to separate the inebriate or naïve from the contents of their wallets.

From late evening until dawn the music pounded and the 'liquid happiness' flowed. It was like one big party in celebration of something significant that nobody could quite recall or care about any longer. This was by far the favourite Friday night destination for Nuru, Lorna and their friends. In their case, as with many others, alcohol was not the fuel they needed for a 'high'. Nor did they wish to partake of any other substance readily available. It was the music, the electrifying atmosphere and the freedom to be themselves in the company of their friends.

Lorna was dating an Arab lad who would drive them to the club but once there, Nuru would leave them to enjoy each other's company. She would either hang out with friends or simply mix with the crowd; she was by now quite gregarious and had no problem with this. Lorna and her boyfriend were probably aware that their relationship was destined to be only for the here and now but they were very fond of each other. He was from a 'well-to-do' family who would expect him to marry a Muslim girl, probably of their choosing, and even if they approved of Lorna, she would have to convert from her family's Christian faith.

Lorna and her boyfriend did fall out from time to time and there would be no lift to the club for the two girls. With the innocence, ignorance, naivety or pure luck of their youth they sometimes resorted to hitching a lift with casual acquaintances they had met at the club. At other times they would accept lifts from total strangers. This was the case on more than one occasion and how they survived without being assaulted, raped or worse is something that Nuru cannot answer to this day.

The alternative venue favoured by the girls was the Yacht Club, also off Langata Road. At weekends, this venue played host to an all-night, open-air disco with a loyal following. Nuru's lift home one evening was on the motorbike of Dominic Kahumbu with whom she had danced the whole night. She had known him some years earlier when they competed in a swimming competition; he represented Nairobi - Nuru, Coast Province. (At that time a photograph of her receiving a medal had appeared in the national press and, naturally, she was dressed in a swimsuit. Local people in Mombasa old town had taken the photo to Mwana Kutani asking how she could allow a Muslim girl to appear in such a garment to which she had replied, "She is in a swimming contest, how else should she dress?" Mwana Kutani was her own person and her father's daughter; nobody was ever left in any doubt about that).

Back then, Nuru had noticed this good-looking, well-groomed

lad and been drawn to him but her interest had been unrequited. This night, however, they discovered a mutual attraction. Neither followed through with it, however...or so she thought.

On an earlier visit she had met Andre, a more mature man with whom she danced late into the night and whom she did arrange to meet later.

When Nuru had quiet moments on her own she would think of her aunt and wonder if she worried about her. She had no idea what her family would be thinking of her. Although her father had clearly thrown her out of his house she really thought of herself as having run away from home and she figured that this would be the way her family would view the situation too.

Whilst at Lorna's, Nuru's mother Aziza had shown up at the hairdressing college with a letter from Mwana Kutani containing three hundred Kenyan Shillings, a sizeable sum at the time. In the letter her aunt expressed concern for her; Aziza said they both were worried for her safety and welfare. But Nuru knew that her mother was not there to take her back to Mombasa because it was clear that she had come to see Nuru without Masoud's approval. Her hands were tied and they both knew it.

Nuru reassured her mother that she would be fine; they hugged and Aziza left with a heavy heart but Nuru understood that her position was impossible. They did not see each other again for several years and that meeting would not be in Kenya.

The morning after Dominic had dropped Nuru off he called at Lorna's house to see her only to be told that Nuru had left and that they did not know where she had gone. This was completely true: that morning she had awoken and made her decision to leave. She said her thanks and goodbyes to the whole family and they assured her that she was very welcome to stay. But her mind was made up. She left early, on foot, with her fairly meagre belongings. They had no knowledge of her plan, if she had one, nor her destination. But Nuru did have a plan, and a destination, and Andre featured largely in it.

Chapter Thirteen

Andre was in his mid-twenties, of Portuguese-Indian extraction. In Kenya he was referred to by the generic term, 'Goan'. Nuru's friends had warned her not to trust him but she was a teenager and not listening to advice, no matter which quarter it came from. He took her to some of the best hotels in town, gave her a roof over her head and promised her the world.

His life seemed to consist of a constant round of meetings and Nuru was frequently taken along. She did not understand his business but she became aware of the term, 'Pyramid Selling'. Only later did she hear others refer to his dealings as a 'Ponzi Scheme'. Although she did not grasp the concept, she could discern by the tone of those using this term that they were not being complimentary about Andre and his business practices. But none of this mattered – Andre told her he loved her and she was living in his apartment in a good degree of comfort.

With little warning he told her he would be leaving for London and would like her to join him on a permanent basis. He would go a few days before her to get organised and she should follow. He gave her a Kenya Airways ticket and left. Nuru was ecstatic at the prospect and told her sister and friends about her good fortune.

Come the day, she packed her belongings, closed the apartment door behind her and left for the airport. She does not recall why she was already holding a valid passport but she duly presented it along with her ticket at the check-in desk. The clerk called her supervisor who asked Nuru where she had obtained the ticket. She gave them Andre's name and was promptly told that she would not be flying anywhere on that ticket – not today nor on any other day: it was from a batch that had recently been stolen from an agent's office. Fortunately for her, they accepted that she had been duped and was an innocent victim. But that was the limit of her good fortune.

Nuru stood devastated at Andre's betrayal, ashamed in front

of the airport staff and excruciatingly embarrassed at the thought of what her friends would think of her. The only person she could call was her sister, Husna, who was staying in a hostel for students at the Kenya Secretarial College. She was not supposed to have guests staying with her but she said Nuru could do so for a couple of days.

Nuru quickly realised that she could not hide from her friends and she was relieved to find that they were universally sympathetic. No one said, "I told you not to trust Andre" but they all voiced their loathing of him and life moved on. She now had to think about how she could pick up the threads of her life and having somewhere to live was obviously the first priority.

Occasionally Nuru would meet some of her friends at the casino. They did not go for the gambling – for her part Nuru could not risk the little money she had and the others had no interest in it. But the bar was a meeting place for a cross section of Nairobi society, much the same as Carnivore.

A friend introduced Nuru to Olav, a German long-term expat in his early thirties who was looking for a live-in child minder for his seven-year-old son. He had divorced the boy's mother but retained custody of the child. Olav had an Ethiopian girlfriend who normally took care of the child but she was on an extended visit to her native country. He intended to partly maintain his alternative care arrangements, which meant that Nuru would not be required at all times. This would leave her time to continue with some of her hairdressing commitments and her studies. She gladly accepted.

Olav had a very comfortable apartment and he kept his girlfriend in considerable luxury. Nuru was in awe of the fine clothing hanging in her closet. On one of her evenings off she could not resist borrowing an embossed T-shirt to go to meet her friends. Unfortunately, they had unwittingly chosen the same venue as Olav that night.

He was drinking with friends when he saw her and recognised the T-shirt. He immediately accused her of stealing and she was shocked at how loud and verbose he was. But it was obvious that Olav had been drinking quite heavily. He was perhaps more openly angry with her than the borrowed T-shirt warranted, but this coincided with another reason he was not happy with Nuru: it seemed that Olav expected her to not only substitute his girlfriend in child minding duties but also in his bed. Her refusal exacerbated the T-shirt event. Nuru and her friends agreed that it would be better if they left for another club.

When Olav arrived home later that night, Nuru was preparing for bed. He entered her room without knocking. Olav was a regular drinker, often drinking to excess, and Nuru was used to seeing him drunk as a result. But his demeanour now, standing in the doorway to her room, was something different, something she hadn't seen before.

At first his voice was quiet and she couldn't make out what he was saying; it may have been German or English – he often switched freely between the two. Whatever it was, he was not coherent. He then moved towards her and, as he raised his voice, she could clearly hear and understand the string of expletives, punctuated by the word 'bitch'.

The oft-drunk Olav that Nuru knew was usually a humorous character, perhaps a little pathetic at times. But she had not seen him like this - she had never seen anyone looking quite this way. His eyes were hard and full of hatred and she could not decide whether this was purely an alcoholic induced episode or something else entirely.

Olav was aware of Nuru's vulnerability. As far as he was concerned, she was alone in Nairobi, virtually a runaway. She had no one to call upon for support or protection, pastoral or otherwise. Perhaps emboldened by alcohol, he had apparently decided that, regardless of Nuru's refusal to accede to his sexual advances, she was living in his home and he was entitled to treat her as he pleased. He had decided that she would do as he demanded.

He was a large man and his strength was now augmented by

anger and the spurious indignation he felt at Nuru's earlier rejection. It was unclear to her how far he was prepared to take his threats – at that moment it seemed he was more than ready and capable of inflicting the violence he was raging about. The verbal abuse, she was sure, was about to turn physical.

It was not so rare in Nairobi for a girl to be found in the street, bruised and broken. Generally, people did not pay too much attention and few would care enough to get involved. In the hours of darkness, such a victim could easily suffer further abuse. Worse still, a lifeless body found on waste ground would spark only cursory enquiries by the police: one of them would be bound to say, "Well you know, she probably had it coming." And likely as not, his colleagues would agree.

Nuru decided to mitigate the pain as best she could. There was nowhere to run to. She knew that screaming was unlikely to elicit any useful response and would most likely intensify his rage. She lay motionless and tried to detach herself from the situation, at least in her mind. She could not fight this brute.

His assault of her was particularly revolting and it disgusted her to the point that she was physically sick afterwards. He was sweaty, slimy and he cursed her the whole time. Even after the attack he continued to curse her. Olav was a nauseating beast of a man.

In submitting, she was not consenting. Nuru was raped as surely as if he had held a knife to her throat. And the way she dealt with that dreadful situation at the time will find empathy with countless victims of rape.

There would be no one to complain to; the police would find the whole thing laughable. She could hear them now:

"Where are the cuts and bruises?"

"Were you not living in his house when this happened?"

"Do you expect us to believe that you have never had sex with him before?" And the spoken or implied assertion, "The only surprise here is that he hadn't exercised his 'right' before now."

She knew her society well: the maxim would be, "A Swahili girl living 'with' a white man in Nairobi was lucky to have been treated so well."

After he left the flat in the morning, Nuru packed her things and walked out into the bustle of Nairobi, homeless once more.

Chapter Fourteen

Prostitution was as commonplace in Nairobi as could be expected of any metropolis. The girls, known locally as 'Malayas', would mix freely with the general crowd at nightspots such as Carnivore. Nuru was on speaking terms with one or two of them and she turned to Fatima to see if she had any ideas about shared accommodation.

Fatima was from the Pakistani community and did not openly flaunt her occupation. But the Carnivore crowd knew what she did for a living and did not judge her.

Nuru now had a modest income from hairdressing and she got some additional funds from ad hoc fashion modelling; enough to contribute towards rent but not enough to rent a place of her own. Fatima suggested she move in with her for a while – she could do with a little help towards expenses.

Without suggesting outright that she should try the same profession, she talked to Nuru about her work. She told her how she did not accede to all demands made by her clients..."Some girls will do anything if the money's right", she said. She told her, "I'm careful about my choice of client but however nice they can be in the beginning, some still feel it's their right to treat you like shit once they are done with you".

She started to show her Modus Operandi to Nuru who had the time to go along with it and it was an amusing insight into an unknown world.

They went to a shop in the jewellery district where Fatima asked to see the owner. She gave him a note saying that she had prepaid for an alteration to the piece of jewellery described in it. The jeweller went to the back of the shop and returned with an envelope allegedly containing the altered item and they left. The envelope contained the cash to pay Fatima's flat and more besides. The subterfuge was conducted in front of the jeweller's wife who remained unaware of his extra-marital arrangements.

There were other similar schemes. She would visit a grocer to buy some small item and pay with a small denomination note. The grocer would give her change for a much larger one.

One day she said Nuru could do a favour for her. She should visit a lawyer at his office to collect some cash. Nuru was glad to help. On arrival at the lawyer's office, however, he invited Nuru in and immediately started removing his clothes. She ran without collecting the cash and Fatima told her that she had better move on.

Some years later Fatima chose the wrong client and was found murdered - just another statistic, perhaps not even that.

In the same apartment block Nuru had befriended another 'Malaya', a Kikuyu lady in her mid-twenties called Grace Chabari. Grace knew that Fatima had tried to introduce Nuru to prostitution and she knew that she had now been asked to leave. She said, "Nuru, this business is not for you and I know you won't do it anyway. Come and help me take care of my little boy – he's eight. You can take him to and from school and feed him when I'm not there. You'll have food and shelter until you can sort something longer term for yourself". Nuru gratefully accepted and stayed with Grace for some weeks. As she grew to know the lady more, so she came to respect her for the dignity she maintained despite her profession. They remained friends for many years.

With her moderate income Nuru started to ask the Carnivore set if they knew of anyone with whom she could share a small flat.

Neil was an English lad of nineteen working for a local commodities trader with whom his father's UK Company did business. The local trader had agreed to take Neil on for a year or so to give him some front line experience of the trade. He had recently broken up with his girlfriend and suggested Nuru could share his two-bedroom flat – no strings attached. Neil had been the one most critical of Andre, warning Nuru in vain to have nothing to do with him. She respected him for that and felt he was being genuine when he said, 'no strings attached' and she moved in.

For many weeks they remained good friends, nothing more, until mutual attraction led them to become a couple. This came as no surprise to the Carnivore set. Neil's ex girlfriend, however, took strong exception. Her name was Rosie and as far as she was concerned they had, as a condition of their parting, a pact not to take up with any of their mutual friends. Nuru only knew Rosie in passing and did not consider her a friend. Rosie did not see it that way. She began telling all who would listen that both Neil and Nuru had 'better watch their backs'.

Rosie was from the Luhya people and it was widely accepted that such a threat should not be taken lightly: The Luhya had a fearsome reputation for exacting harsh revenge on their perceived enemies.

Neil made sure that Nuru did not move around Nairobi alone when he could not escort her and their friends from Carnivore did their best to protect them too.

One evening, Nuru and Neil were having dinner at the Mount Kenya Safari Club when Rosie stormed up to their table. In Swahili she burst forth with a stream of obscenities about what she was going to do to them – mostly directed at Neil. She warned them that they had better watch their backs and left, completely oblivious to the dismay she had caused staff and customers alike.

Rosie was well known to the security guards at Neil's apartment complex and so it was that the following day she was able to reach the door to his apartment without his prior notice. As he answered the door she kicked it open sending him stumbling backwards across the room. Nuru ran to the bathroom and held the door closed; there was no lock. She could hear Rosie screaming like a banshee, breaking glass and ornaments as they came to hand. Neil was being attacked ferociously and there was nothing Nuru could do about it.

The noise was such that other residents could not fail to be alerted and so too the security staff who came to Neil's rescue, throwing the screaming, thrashing Rosie into the street.

Nuru emerged to find Neil with deep gouges to his face, arms and chest inflicted by Rosie's nails. They were thankful she had not armed herself with a knife or broken bottle – often a weapon of choice. They became even more vigilant now.

In February 1985 Neil told Nuru that his contract in Nairobi was ending and he would be returning to the UK. He said he loved her and wanted her to come with him but he did not have access to enough funds to buy her a ticket. He was due to fly with Kenya Airways.

She said that she didn't want to lie to him – she didn't love him the same way he did her but she believed she might grow to do so in time. If he still wanted her to go with him they must try to work something out. He accepted her position, appreciated her honesty and strongly reaffirmed his wish that she come with him. They had a little time before his departure date and set about exploring ways to obtain a ticket for Nuru.

Neil discovered that for a little more than the price of his ticket with Kenya Airways he could get two economy seats with Aeroflot. They would fly in March.

Nuru took the bus to Mombasa to visit her aunt before leaving. She told her that she had met her Mzungu, a good man who said he loved her. He accepted her knowing that the love he had for her was not fully returned. Mwana Kutani blessed her and told her she must follow her dream.

Neil telephoned his father to tell him, in a very light-hearted manner, that he would be bringing a souvenir home with him. Nuru was unaware of his father's reaction at the other end of the line.

In March, twenty-year-old Neil and eighteen-year-old Nuru boarded a plane taking them on a twenty-two hour flight to London via Cairo, Leningrad and Moscow. Nuru had never felt cold like it.

What neither of them knew at the time was that there was a third passenger on the flight with them. Nuru was expecting Neil's baby.

Part Two

A Souvenir from Kenya

Chapter Fifteen

I arrived at London's Heathrow Airport underdressed for a cool morning in March. I didn't possess clothes for this climate.

Neil's father, Jack, greeted us warmly and did his best to put me at ease. It worked to some extent. He showed no surprise at my being the 'souvenir' Neil had joked about on the phone.

I climbed into the back of Jack's Jaguar whilst Neil sat next to Jack. Both men made sure I was not excluded from the conversation, even though they had a lot to catch up on: Neil had been in Kenya for more than a year with the limited communications of the era. No Skype or Facetime back then and people were not frivolous about making international calls, regardless of their finances.

As soon as we left the immediate environs of the airport, the air, no longer infused with jet fumes, tasted clear and fresh. In Kenya, familiarity meant that I no longer noticed the rich, earthy mustiness that Neil said he loved so much. But a blind person taking one breath of English air could not have failed to notice they were no longer in Africa.

We passed along well maintained highways into streets finished with even pavements, the houses in straight lines with tended gardens inside well-built brick walls or wooden fences. Even the hedgerows along the lane that Jack used as a short cut were neatly trimmed back. Everything was orderly and it looked as if it had always been this way.

None of this came as a surprise to me – I didn't arrive as a wide-eyed immigrant. Over many years I'd seen the photographs my friends brought back from visits to London, the US, Canada and Europe so everything looked much as I had expected. But I was thrilled to be here at last.

The family home in Pinner, west of London, was spacious with a large garden and a pool. Jack's wife, Ann, greeted me courteously but not with the same warmth shown by her husband. She showed me where I would be sleeping – the room vacated by Neil's brother Mark, who was on extended travels somewhere abroad. There was no discussion about Neil's and my current sleeping arrangements: this was the way it would be here in the family home. (Fortunately, there were no creaking floorboards between Neil's room and my own…)

Ann had gone to great lengths to lay-on a delicious homecoming lunch. What I remember most is the roast chicken and my introduction to English mustard. I assumed it to be the same as the American version and spread it liberally over the meat on my plate. I was used to chilli with my food but this was a different experience. I ate it all without any outward signs of discomfort, but I was exploding inside. The table was laid with silver cutlery and fine cut glass for what I learned later was an excellent wine. I partook of the wine freely without a thought for any impression my indulgence may or may not have given.

I was awakening to the fact that the Pattersons were quite wealthy, something I had not considered or discussed with Neil. In Kenya he didn't spend wildly although we lived and ate very well. We also lived in a comfortable flat in the fashionable Westlands district but money had never meant anything to me: I only needed enough to live on and to have fun. In any event, when it came to travelling back to the UK, it was obvious that Neil had only limited funds; he never gave the impression that he or his family was rich. But I was beginning to understand that these people were, without doubt, pretty well off.

Almost immediately after our arrival Neil took up a junior position at the company where his father was a senior director and shareholder. This meant that I was soon alone with his mother for most of the day. She continued to be polite and, realising I had no suitable attire for the English climate, brought several items of warm clothing including a coat to my room. During the day I would ask if I could help with anything from ironing to cooking. Throughout my life in Kenya I was used to playing an active part in the running of the home and it came naturally to me that I should continue to do so here in Pinner. Always, Ann would tell me that there was no need. To Neil, however, she portrayed me as lazy: she said, "She sits all day and never offers to help with anything." To his credit, Neil defended me. But the friction was building and it was clear that living under the same roof was not going to work out well for any of us.

After six weeks or so it was becoming too much for any of us to bear. It was clear that, to Neil's mother I was not an acceptable long – or even medium – term proposition as far as her son was concerned. And she didn't seem to mind that I should be aware of this. The days when we were in the house together would have been excruciating had I not spent most of the time in my room or at least not in the same room as Ann. Neil told me that he was never good enough in his mother's eyes so I would have little chance of faring any better.

His father was aware of the situation and thankfully came to our rescue. His company had a lease on a five-bedroom penthouse in Ivory House, St. Catherine's dock, next to the Tower of London. It was placed at Neil's disposal and we didn't need any encouragement to move there.

Neil stored his E-type at the family home and drove us to our new home in his 'everyday' car – a gold Porsche 924 that his father had presented him with on his return to the UK.

The first night in the penthouse I sat on the toilet and thought about what was happening to me. I was grateful, of course. I was elated, obviously. But I was also confused and out of my depth. However, I had the optimism and invincibility of youth. I was going to enjoy the moment and let life take its course. This was way beyond my youthful dreams. But I did feel that I was growing to love Neil as he did me. He protected me and defended me even in the face of his own mother's attempts to denigrate me.

We discussed my pregnancy in practical terms. As we saw it, so much was happening to us - our lives were full of uncertainties at this point. We decided that neither of us was prepared to bring a child into this scenario and I arranged to have an abortion.

Saying it now, it sounds as though it was a light-hearted, selfish decision taken easily; it was not at all like that. We discussed it over several days before making the appointment and by then we felt certain that it was the right thing for us – and for the unborn child. At least that was what we thought at that time.

I have no recollection of second thoughts once the final decision was made. But later, and even today, there are times when I question that decision. I can still get a pang of guilt and a sense of loss. But what is done, is done.

Chapter Sixteen

Even in the face of Ann's attitude towards me I admired her and wanted to love her as a mother and be loved in return. It was never to be that way. My admiration came from watching her set off at least twice weekly to do her voluntary work. She attended the dying at the hospice or in their home to manicure their nails for them. She did other voluntary work besides.

Wishing to love her and be loved by her was symptomatic of a fault line running through both Neil's and my own personalities – we were prone to placing our love and looking for love and approval in the wrong places. Notwithstanding, I believe I did my best to live up to Ann's expectations – not that I was quite sure what those were.

I also had certain sympathy for Ann; perhaps she couldn't help the way she was towards Neil or me. She had a sister in Wales and Ann described how their mother, Vera, always favoured her sister over her. Ann could do no right in Vera's eyes; her sister could do no wrong. Neil's brother, Mark, was wayward on many counts but remained the apple of his mother's eye. Neil could only look to his father for approval. I watched history repeating itself.

There were many aspects of my own family's behaviour open to question. Outsiders, especially those from a different culture, might find the ways of my father, mother, stepmother, and others, peculiar in the extreme. And they could be right. Now I was the outsider and I was finding some of the ways of my English hosts interesting to observe.

Within the confines of the home, with only family present, Ann constantly disrespected Jack whereas he only ever treated her well and with deference. It was general knowledge that, to a great extent, they led separate lives and that she and Jack slept apart. No one ever spoke of it of course. Against this background, I couldn't help but admire the way the family continued to conduct their public lives with such civility towards each other. To the outside world, all was normal. This seemed to be the English way that I had heard about – indiscretions were swept under the carpet. 'Don't wash your dirty linen in public', was a phrase I came to know later.

Neil was doing well at his work and the company was very successful. The family regularly entertained clients at the finest restaurants, clubs and hotels in London and I became used to dressing well. I needed no tuition in how to conduct myself on such occasions.

One of the first I recall was a trade dinner at Grosvenor House Hotel on Park Lane. The vast ballroom with its sparkling chandeliers was set up with round tables seating ten or twelve. I was next to the Ugandan Ambassador and his wife. I was a fast learner and if I had any doubts about a cuisine new to me I would watch others before proceeding as if it was something I ate every day. (A very kind waiter at The St. James Club quietly – and without demeaning me in any way by his tone – pointed out that Camembert has a silent 'T'. I appreciated that.)

Practically every morning Ann would phone me at the flat to ask what I was going to give Neil to eat. I found this infuriating – did she think that all I was capable of cooking was African bush-meat and rice? I remained civil about it but a friend told me I should tell her he would be getting pussy for breakfast, pussy for lunch and pussy for dinner. How tempted I was!

She also continuously asked Neil when I would be returning to Kenya. He quickly tired of this constant nagging and after a couple of months he said to his mother, "She isn't going back – I'm going to marry her." He had already proposed and I had accepted. There was no doubt in my mind about Neil's sincerity but hearing him say that to his mother made the prospect startlingly real. I felt so happy – I could now allow myself the luxury of thinking about my future.

The apartment at Ivory House was always a temporary measure. By September of my first year in London we took a lease on a flat in Pennybank Chambers on the corner of Great Eastern and Old Streets in the City of London, close to Liverpool Street Station. With one bedroom, a bathroom, a small kitchen, and a living room it did not compare to the spacious apartment at Ivory House. But we loved it and it was ours.

I arrived in the UK on a six-month visa and had extended it for a further six without problem. Neil's mother had progressed from complaining that I did 'nothing to help in Pinner' and 'when was I going back to Kenya' to 'when was I going to get a job' - which she asked Neil with monotonous regularity. She was deliberately obtuse in her disregard for the fact that I had no work permit. I didn't need Ann's nagging to spur me on to find work but without a permit my options were greatly diminished.

On the ground level of Pennybank Chambers was a small grocery, newsagent and tobacconist – a typical corner shop run by an Asian family. They understood my dilemma and kindly agreed that I could work if I was prepared to take payment in toilet rolls, tissues, soap and cigarettes. I was happy just to be able to do something useful with my days. A German lady called Elke called in every morning for a newspaper and her Dunhills, en route to work around the corner.

Harvey's wine bar was not part of the large, well-known group, it was owned by Elke with her Italian business partner, Giovanni. (Elke was divorced but she visited her ex-husband in prison on Fridays to take him some comforts. I heard he was serving a long sentence for armed robbery). She was always very kindly towards me and she asked if I would like to work in the wine bar. She said, "Don't worry about the work permit problem, I'll take care to pay you your wages and if anyone asks, you're a friend's daughter just visiting and helping out to get some work experience." The Asian family gave me their blessing and I started behind the bar.

Giovanni did his best to teach me and he was very patient. I wasn't serving, just opening bottles and pouring drinks. After a couple of weeks Elke called me into her office. "You're hopeless behind the bar," she said, and I thought I'd be shown the door. Instead she told me she was sure I would do better as a waitress. She said, "The girls will help you get used to it and I'm sure you'll do well."

Harvey's attracted the City traders; this was around the time someone coined the phrase 'Yuppie' – Young, upwardly mobile professional. 'The City', as London's financial district is known, was male dominated even more so then than now and the wine bar clientele had long lunches and fat expense accounts. Business 'entertaining' wasn't just acceptable, it was considered indispensable – an absolute necessity. And 'wining and dining' clients was in full swing.

I worked with Helen, from Ireland and Patricia, an East-End girl. They were hard workers, knew their business, and knew their clientele. Neither took any nonsense but they created a great atmosphere full of banter, innuendo and double entendre. The customers loved them, stayed long and spent heavily.

I was a bit fearful at first that the girls may be hostile towards me for encroaching on their 'patch', but not a bit of it. They were friendly, patient and very helpful and they trained me well. They taught me 'Silver Service', which was the style at Harvey's – not to be found in a wine bar I can think of these days. I dressed smartly, as did they, and soon got to know the 'regulars'.

Catering establishments in the City closed at weekends along with the financial markets and most didn't stay open late in the evening either. This made for very acceptable working hours and didn't impinge on Neil's and my social life in the least. The exception was the run up to Christmas when spending in places like Harvey's rocketed and they stayed open for dinner as well as lunch. I was kept very busy and I loved it.

When service was finished it was usual for Elke and Giovanni to invite the staff to have a drink or two and some food with them. Sometimes Neil would drop in and join us. I got the feeling that he wasn't really happy about this 'second family' scenario. I felt that there was an underlying jealousy or possessiveness going on. I had the definite impression that he didn't like me in a situation that I had made for myself, one over which he had no influence or control. But he didn't complain too loudly and we had some fun times together. Well, I enjoyed them at least.

After some months, Ursula, a Polish girl who lived in a council flat somewhere in Islington, joined the team. She was an extremely driven character, determined to drag herself out of the hand-to-mouth existence she had at the time. She planned to do this by improving her education and through sheer hard work.

Tips were pooled but the two 'old hands' thought that they should take a larger share than Ursula and me. I would probably have accepted it but Ursula would have none of it: "We do the same work, we take the same tip," she said. And she had a way of saying things so that people didn't argue with her. She was always telling me to, "look after number one – make your own way and push yourself." She had a hard life but despite living where she did, she sent her daughter, Olivia, to a private school. She got involved in all kinds of little ventures to make ends meet. Every week, Ursula had a new way to make money. She would arrive at work with kitchen appliances, car parts or leather jackets – all at a bargain price of course. She was determined to hustle so that she could to make a life for herself and her daughter. She amused me and I admired her guts and tenacity.

As part of Ursula's determination that I should be strong, independent and push myself in life, she urged me to learn to drive and eventually I did. As a result, when later we moved to an apartment further from the wine bar, Neil gave me his gold Porsche 924 whilst he drove a silver 944 bought for him by his mother. It was quite ludicrous that I would drive to work in the Porsche and park it in a garage behind the restaurant– probably costing a large chunk of my earnings for the day. But I didn't need the money, just the job. At that time some of the younger customers would ask me where I lived and what I drove. They were shocked at the answers and if they doubted me I would tell them where they could see the car parked close by.

Chapter Seventeen

I came to understand that Neil was a control freak. He regularly chose my dresses and shoes and I didn't complain: he had good taste, shopped at the best stores and I was grateful for the beautiful things he bought for me to wear. But he would also tell me what I should wear on each occasion.

I remember once after we were married he organized a birthday treat for me. We were booked on the Orient Express from London to Liverpool for the Grand National. Neil bought me a very stylish, blue, designer trouser-suit but there was something not quite right about it – too short, too long or too tight, I don't recall. He agreed I should take it back and change it.

The shop was in Beauchamp Place, Knightsbridge, just along from Harrods. The owner suggested I look around for a replacement and I found a dress I liked very much. I was then informed that it was £1,000 or so, whereas the trouser-suit was around £750. I had credit cards to pay the difference but thought I should first call Neil for his approval. He agreed – with some words of caution about how I should look after it.

At the Grand National we had an ice cream whilst we went to the paddock to look at the horses and I managed to spill some on my £1,000 dress. Neil was apoplectic and told me where to take it to have it cleaned – a company in Bond Street with a royal crest. This was no High-Street cleaner - and there was nothing 'High Street' about the bill either! It was strange: he was undoubtedly generous towards me and my wardrobe was beyond anything I could have imagined such a short time before. But he could be thrown into a spin by a simple mistake on my part. And when it happened it would invariably be related to my couture. Neil did not, however, choose my wedding dress.

Once Ann accepted that he was serious about marrying me, she took complete control. She didn't consult me on anything. This was going to be a Pattersons wedding and she would make all the arrangements. She took me to Pronuptia in Mayfair and selected my dress. In fairness to her she did her best to make me feel that it was my final choice but she had good taste and it was a classic style. I felt wonderful in it.

What follows here and in the next chapter is not as flippant as it now sounds.

I am acutely aware of the solemnity of religion and I had no wish to disrespect either Islam or the Christian Church. My view has long been that the two religions have more in common than divides them. The problem, as I see it, is that the followers of both seem unable to rise above their differences. I repeat, in the strongest possible terms, that I did not and do not intend disrespect to either – but neither do I wish to align myself with one or the other whilst bigotry and dogma divides them. My moral compass in this respect is very clear in my mind.

Without consulting anyone else, Neil and I figured that I would need to convert to Christianity in order to be married in church in accordance with his parents' wishes. In my ignorance – and Neil didn't guide me otherwise – I approached the nearest church in Great Eastern Street in order to take Bible lessons. I attended several lessons before we started to consider the fact that this was a Catholic church and Neil was, ostensibly at least, Church of England.

In the event, a kindly, pragmatic Vicar, with whom we discussed the whole subject, readily agreed to marry us. He told us we would make our vows in front of the same God who prevailed over both religions and we would do so in his church in the Parish of Eastcote in West London. The date for the wedding was set for 15 February 1986 – my father's birthday. I was nineteen, Neil twenty-one.

I recall arriving at the church accompanied by Jack and as the car door opened, for the first time, reality struck me. However, at the same time, it all seemed surreal. It was as though I was a spectator watching the scene play out before me. I have little recollection of the ceremony itself; I was in a bit of a trance, acting out my role in a dream. It was purely a state of mind, completely internalised, for no one ever mentioned afterwards that they had noticed anything strange about my demeanour. But it remains vague, like the memory of a dream after waking.

Ann chose to wear white to our wedding – evidently it didn't matter that our dresses were the same colour on this occasion. On a previous occasion, when meeting at our flat for pre-lunch drinks, Ann had insisted that I change my dress because she had arrived in one of much the same colour. I don't remember caring much about such trivia on my wedding day. But I did care that she didn't really want me to be her son's bride.

The reception was held at Grim's Dyke Hotel near Harrow, a beautiful country house where we had dined as a family on special occasions. Formerly it had been the home of W.S. Gilbert of Gilbert and Sullivan fame and to this day their operas are often performed there. It had also been used as a film set for various period pieces and other works.

I give all credit to Neil's mother – the arrangements were faultless and Jack made sure the reception was lavish but tasteful. A harpist played and we had well-made minestrone followed by delicious beef wellington. It all went without a hitch.

Apart from Neil's family, guests included some neighbours we had come to know and the team from the wine bar. I invited a cousin, whom I knew wouldn't judge the Muslim girl having a Christian wedding. A girlfriend and her daughter accompanied her. I should say there were about eighty people in total. We invited two sisters who lived close to us. The younger of the two got drunk whenever we saw them; she didn't disappoint. I got on well with Jack's father, Andrew, a lovely man, and his sister Jean – she always had a smile and a kind heart. Her husband, George, was mostly quiet but a nice man once you got him chatting. Ann's relatives were also nice people and I found her mother, Vera, particularly likeable. Ann's sister, Joan, was very bright and bubbly, married to Martin, a lover of cigars. (Martin wore the most awful toupee - the quality improved only later after he sold his rubber company.) It was a grand day.

My visa status was such that I couldn't leave and re-enter the country for 6 months after the wedding. This was to prove that it was not a sham for the purpose of obtaining resident's status. So Jack booked a lovely suite for us at London's 'Inn on the Park' for our wedding night.

I changed into a white leather skirt and white top with grey and white leather panels. Neil had great taste in clothes. Waiting for us in the room was chilled Champagne and chocolate-covered strawberries. Neil and I enjoyed watching boxing together and to our delight Barry McGuigan was fighting Danilo Cabrera so we settled down to watch. We always interacted well together whilst watching boxing and it was a lot of fun.

This doesn't sound like much of a wedding night, I know. The problem was, I was still feeling disgusted with myself following the abortion and our sex-life was non-existent. Neil was very understanding and supportive and I will always admire him for that.

Despite this rather odd start to our married life, we were now Mr. and Mrs. Patterson and we truly loved each other. Life had changed so dramatically for me in such a short period of time and I was extremely grateful to Neil, as well as his family, including his mother. In different ways they had all made such an immense impact on my life and I really did appreciate it. Most of all, I was now married to Neil – not just any Mzungu but the best I could have wished for.

Chapter Eighteen

I learned from my aunt that before my marriage had become general knowledge throughout the family, my stepmother, Rehema, had been delighting in telling everyone that I had gone to London, 'to make prostitution'. She claimed to know, as a matter of fact, that Neil, 'the Mzungu', was my pimp. Nobody needs a stepmother like that. My marriage should have shamed her enormously in front of the family but Rehema was quite thick-skinned. Afterwards she was sweet as sugar towards me but I had long-since seen through her hypocrisy.

I sent photographs of the wedding to my aunt in Mombasa but I'd been careful not to include any taken outside the church. Neil and I discussed the expectations of my family back in Kenya – as far as they knew we had a Registry Office wedding and what remained now was to complete the process in the eyes of Islam. How should we do this with a marriage certificate bearing the name of the Reverend David Malcolm Hollingwood Hayes and Neil, a child of his Parish?

I'm not proud of the conspiracy that ensued but none of it was for our own sakes. It was the only way we saw to placate the feelings of my family in Kenya – not to seek their approval but to spare their hurt.

The Marriage Certificate was the first problem to overcome and my Polish workmate, Ursula, provided the solution in her inimitable fashion. She had been married in a registry office. She would take a copy of her certificate, substitute our names for hers and her husband's, change the date and we would have what we needed. I flinched at the casual way she undertook the task but went along with it.

The Vicar had been very accommodating where my religion was concerned but I felt quite sure that there was no chance of an Imam in Mombasa, or anywhere else, solemnising my marriage to a Christian boy. Neither of us believed in religion, be it Christianity,

Islam, or any other. But neither did we look down on those who wished to believe. As far as we were concerned, it was purely a matter of personal choice.

Neil decided that he should at least understand the rudiments of what it meant to be a Muslim so that he could discuss the subject in an informed manner with my family, should the occasion arise. We felt sure there would be pressure on him to convert in order to dignify the marriage in the eyes of Islam. So, without commitment, he undertook to study the basics of the religion.

We spoke to an elder at a Mosque in the East End who was very understanding: Here was a Christian boy who had 'married' a Muslim girl. For the moment, the man was prepared to ignore the past tense - It was not a marriage as far as he was concerned, even if we had a piece of paper that said it was. It would be counterproductive, at this stage, to dwell upon the resultant immorality of our relationship; the 'future husband' wished to understand his 'future wife's' religion, nothing more right now.

Neil took his informal lessons seriously and with due deference for his mentor: he would never undertake anything without giving himself fully to the task, neither would he be disrespectful of others' beliefs. He only ever intended to understand the fundamentals and he was a fast learner. Afterwards he told me that it was all very friendly and the clerics he met were charming people. He never deceived them by confirming that he would convert to the faith. And they never applied undue pressure – he was left to decide for himself. We both respected them enormously for this.

From the time we were in a position to make our own decisions about religion, we had both decided that we did not believe in the faith followed by our respective families. This is not to say that we disrespected their right to believe, follow, or devote themselves to their religions, just that religion was not for us and we did not believe in it. This did not change for either of us.

I sent the 'marriage certificate' prepared by Ursula to my aunt.

As far as I know, she organised representatives to attend the Mosque close to her home in Mombasa – an all-male affair. I have no idea what the procedure involved but now everyone was happy that the marriage was real. And so it was. Neil's knowledge of Islam was never put to the test. Wherever she may be, I hope my aunt can understand and forgive me.

Shortly after the wedding my mother suggested she should come to London to visit us. Mwana Kutani and others told her that she should not visit newlyweds so soon but she wouldn't listen. On her arrival I took her to our flat in Pennybank Chambers and said, "As you can see, mum, it's only a small, one-bedroom place not at all suitable for you to stay. I'll take you to cousin's place in Islington. It's much larger and it's close-by so we can meet up." This turned out to be a good decision even though she did her best to make me feel awful about it.

She stayed a month during which time she told anyone prepared to listen how she had not been allowed to stay with her own daughter. I wondered if she might have spared a thought for the time she didn't hesitate to throw me out of her house at the age of 11 simply for putting too much salt in the meatballs! Her negativity drove everyone nuts over the course of that month and I can't say I was sorry to see her leave.

The six months of visa restriction soon passed and we were free to travel.

Our first trip as Mr. & Mrs. Patterson was to visit my aunt to introduce Neil. It was important to both of us that she should meet him as soon as possible. So in the autumn of 1986 we booked flights for Kenya. Although we flew into Nairobi, I had no desire to see my father. We hired a car and drove to Mombasa to give us both a chance to re-familiarize ourselves with the country we both loved.

Having booked into the Nyali Beach Hotel we set off for Mombasa Old Town. Driving through those familiar streets, my childhood came flooding back. We parked the car outside the place we used to call 'Hoteli' on the Old Kilindini Road. It was just a snack bar and why we called it 'Hoteli' I have no idea. I wanted to walk Neil through the streets of the Old Town to Mwana Kutani's house to give him a feel for the place where I had grown up.

I avoided the road where the Washihiri people – a generic term used for those of Yemeni descent – used to make charcoal. The whole street was blackened by the dust and as children we would look for small pieces of charcoal, sometimes for drawing and sometimes to make our own little fires in the afternoon when the adults were sleeping. We would take a Karai – the small double handled bowl we are now more familiar with as a Balti – and perhaps a potato or some other vegetables from home and cook a snack in the street. We did it for our amusement rather than any need of nourishment.

We would also pick up discarded bottle tops, drill a hole in four and insert twigs to make toy cars to play with. Life was pretty simple but I have only happy memories of those afternoons in the streets of the Old Town. And now Neil and I strolled the same streets as I described the smells and sounds of my youth: Charcoal being burnt for cooking; the sweet smell of cakes from the bakers, usually Pakistanis or Bangladeshis. They would make Kaimati, a crisp pancake covered in sugar. I told Neil how we would sometimes pass by the shop on the roundabout on Moi Avenue after school to pick up a pie filled with spiced, minced beef and onions.

Now we could smell Udi – literally translated it means Aloes but the name was used for essences of various scents. Ladies would make a tripod, take a small burner into which they would put their chosen Udi, and hang their dress over it whilst they got ready to go out in the evening. It would also be used as a room fragrance. There was a particular one used in the Madrasa known as Ubani – literally, perfume – and this would be burnt during the making of a Dua – a prayer.

I recounted the smells that would fill the air after dark during Ramadan. Stalls were set up along Abdel Nasser Road running north from the MacKinnon Market offering many different delights: mshikake (skewers) with spiced meat cooked on charcoal; mkate wa nyama which roughly translates to 'meatloaf'. It was actually a thin pastry, folded with mincemeat and an egg inside and fried; kai mati - dough dropped into deep fat then soaked in syrup. The oil and syrup together would run out when you bit into them! Cut lesi was spiced mincemeat with mashed potato around like a scotch egg.

I told Neil how on Sundays we may go to the Lighthouse area to stroll and play and maybe buy some cassava, fried and topped with chilli and lemon or made into crisps. Less exotic perhaps was the Lyons Maid ice cream we might get from the seller on his bicycle with the cool-box on the front.

The sounds of the Old Town were all around us too. We could hear the call of a 'Mali Mali' trader in a street nearby. He would be pushing his two-wheeled cart calling "mali mali" (literally, property or goods). People would be coming from their houses with unwanted dresses and other items to part-exchange for the pots, pans, utensils and trinkets that would be on the cart. They were always items that could not be found in the local shops.

As we passed one house we could hear the sound of wailing for a deceased loved one; another was filled with the sound of a wedding celebration. I could clearly visualize myself here as a child, perhaps laughing at a friend chasing a stray chicken in the hope of taking a nice prize home. How I loved this place.

How lucky I had been to be brought up here by Mwana Kutani. She was waiting for us in her seat by the door as usual.

My emotions on seeing her again were raw; I loved and admired this lady so much and she returned that love unconditionally. To our relief she welcomed Neil without reservation. He wasn't the typical boy she would have preferred me to marry: Muslim, a second cousin perhaps, but she showed no sign of disappointment. He quickly came under her spell, as did all who met that amazing lady.

I ached to tell her the truth about our wedding but the whole matter was now settled and we could see how happy she was. There was no way that I was going to destroy the illusion, having perpetrated such an elaborate ploy. I comforted myself with the contentment and approval etched on her face; I could live with this. Then she said she wanted to talk to Neil alone so I went outside.

Afterwards, he told me that she thanked him passionately for 'saving her daughter'. I always considered her to be my mother and she in turn loved me and raised me as her own daughter. She told him she had worried about what would become of me in Nairobi and she was grateful to Neil for taking me away and giving me a chance in life.

We stayed for a couple of weeks and went to places in Mombasa that I had no experience of in my youth. Sometimes we ate at the Tamarind on the cliff across the creek from Kaloleni, a bit north of Old Town. It's a hotel with a great restaurant on a terrace looking over the Creek to Mombasa Island. They serve very good, fresh fish. Even if it existed when I was a child, it certainly didn't figure in anyone's thinking that I knew in those days.

One day we gathered up the younger cousins and took them to the new Water Park in Nyali. They talked about their day out long after and I felt thrilled that we were able to do that for them.

On subsequent trips we did the whole tourist thing including Safaris but even if we saw nobody else, we always made time to visit my aunt.

Chapter Nineteen

At the time, I suppose my life in London, both prior and subsequent to our marriage, seemed normal, even average to me. I was aware that my colleagues at Harvey's didn't enjoy the same lifestyle but on the other hand I met plenty people who did. Indeed, because of the circles that Neil's family moved in, I knew many who seemed to do little other than travel and socialize much more extravagantly than us. What I'm saying is that it had all become a kind of norm.

However, I took nothing for granted. I always remembered that things could have been so different for me had I not met Neil and his family. I have expressed my reservations about Ann and I'm not sure if that says more about her or about me. But she was always very generous to me. My problem, if I can call it a problem, was that I placed very little store by material things, which is probably why I treated my surroundings and lifestyle so casually: they were superficial. What I really sought was Ann's love and acceptance. I don't believe I ever achieved that goal.

My life with Neil, however, was enviable by most people's standards and I did enjoy it to the full. In a lot of ways we were very compatible and enjoyed our life and adventures together. But Neil had quirks in his nature that I was never able to understand. As a consequence, incidents would occasionally arise where our respective points of view were diametrically opposed. Some, I was never able to fathom, even in the cold light of day.

Neil's work often took him overseas and sometimes I accompanied him. But his trips were frequent which meant I would often be left alone in London; I didn't mind at all. We had moved to a new larger flat and I felt very secure. I was never intimidated by the city.

I remember one of his visits was to Amsterdam and, somewhat chauvinistically, he arranged for a close friend to take me to dinner on the first night. He was charming, witty and a good companion for the evening. We dined well, went to a club and danced and he escorted me home in a most gentlemanly manner. He had driven to collect me and his car was parked outside the flat; he now intended to drive home. We had been drinking steadily for the whole evening and I told him that driving was definitely not an option - especially as he had quite evidently drunk more than me. We had two bedrooms so I said he should stay the night, adding, "I'm sure Neil would agree."

    Even though the alcohol had clouded his judgment as far as driving was concerned, he now hesitated at the thought of whether Neil really would have agreed had he been asked the question. Common sense prevailed however, and he came inside. Without either a nightcap or coffee I showed him his facilities for the night and he duly retired to the spare bedroom.

    As I was about to get into bed myself, Neil phoned to ask how was my evening. I told him where we had been and how charming his friend had been. I then told him that his friend had a little too much to drink to drive home so he was sleeping in our spare room.

    Oh my goodness! He went crazy on the phone: "How could you even think of allowing him to stay? What the hell will my colleagues say when they know he stayed the night with you?" And so on.

    I explained that, to me, it was pure logic: "You must have trusted your friend to take me out for the evening so why is there now a problem? I've saved him from driving when he shouldn't. And anyway, we have a spare room, why wouldn't you want your friend to use it?"

    My argument failed to assuage his disapproval but his pal was sound asleep in the other room and I wasn't going to throw him out at this stage. From the start, I thought it very odd that Neil should arrange for me to be escorted for the evening but I went along with it. "Why not?" I thought. But he didn't make any similar arrangements after that.

    Dining out, with or without the family, was a regular feature of our lives. I loved the places we went to – Greek clubs, the theatre, the Bolshoi Ballet, Musicals, Cabarets and hotels where you could dance to great bands during dinner. We regularly ate at some of the finest private dining venues in and around London. Quite often it would be at the behest of Jack and Ann and of course, that would include lunches and dinners at the family home in Pinner.

I use the term at their 'behest' advisedly. I found it amusing when at times Neil would come off the phone from his mother and say something like, "We're going to Mum and Dad's for lunch on Sunday; it's a Wills job." This was a little pressure that Ann liked to apply, albeit through the proxy of her husband, if she thought there was any chance of resistance to their 'invitation'. Before Neil could excuse us from the gathering Jack would say, "Now you must be here Neil, it's a Wills job you know," followed by a mitigating chuckle. The meaning, of course, was that if we didn't attend they would consider cutting him out of their Will.

At these gatherings there was always a lot of discussion not only about family and business matters but political and global topics too. The aspect common to all was that I was never included in the conversation. I was hardly ever asked for an opinion and on the rare occasion that I might be, Neil would answer for me. I will accept that I may have had little to contribute to the business matters but I always had an awareness of what was going on in the world. I would have appreciated a glimmer of interest in my opinion at times.

Our first holiday abroad as a family was to Barbados sometime in 1987. Neil's brother, Mark, joined us with his girlfriend, Christine. Jack rented a house on the Sandy Lane estate called Dar-es-Salaam. Previous guests, according to the guest book, had included Keith Richards of the Rolling Stones, so there was nothing shabby about the place. And we had access to a Cabana at Sandy Lane Hotel – then, as now, the most prestigious spot on the island.

Back then Barbados had not been developed to the extent it has been these days. None of the now-famous restaurants had been established and Sandy Lane had not been redeveloped into the glorious establishment that adorns the West Coast today. There were a few smart restaurants - Bagatelle, Carambola, La Maison, Coco's and L'Cage aux Folles come to mind. They were very good but they have been supplanted by a plethora of others where considerable investment has been injected with impressive results.

The next holiday was the five of us, without Christine. We flew British Airways First Class and were collected by limo at JFK New York to be taken to an amazing property in The Hamptons. From what I have already said I am aware that I have given the impression that I found it very easy to assimilate this incredible lifestyle. At first I really did think that I was taking it all in my stride, but it wasn't strictly true. You would need to be something special, odd perhaps, to come from my life in Nairobi to this 'routine' luxury without missing a beat in the transition.

During our stay at the Hamptons, we were out for dinner most, if not every, evening and the strain started to tell on me. I began to realise just how isolated I felt in a world completely alien to me. It had nothing to do with my colour or race; I didn't feel inferior or separate in that way. It was the opulence on an everyday basis that I was starting to struggle with. This really was a surreal existence and I was beginning to feel uncomfortable with it. And it was starting to show.

Neil quickly picked up on my sadness and arranged for us to go to stay at Mark's apartment in Downtown New York for a few days. He made a huge effort to make me feel at ease and to put a smile back on my face. It worked; we had a great time.

Sometime in 1987 I raised the subject of us having children. After a difficult start to our marriage, normal sexual relations had resumed and life seemed so much more settled than it had in the early days. Initially, Neil was not keen on the idea and he remained so for quite a while.

Quite bizarrely, he arrived home one day with two Amazonian

Parrots purchased from Harrods exotic pets department. They seemed happy together in their enormous cage. Tongue-in-cheek, Neil said, "Let's see how you get on with looking after these and then perhaps we can discuss babies"

Have a longhaired dog that sheds fur everywhere, if you must. Have a cat that sharpens its claws on your furniture. But don't have a Parrot. And never have two. These guys ate – or attempted to eat – everything. Nothing was out of bounds to them when they were uncaged. Remote controls were wrecked, replaced and wrecked again. Beaks were honed on tables, chairs, doors and doorframes, cruets, kitchen utensils and ornaments. Nothing was sacred.

For some reason we named Neil's 'Grumpy' and mine 'Sweetie'. Neil would arrive home and say to me, "Hello sweetie" as he came through the door. 'Sweetie' would join in with several repetitions of "Hello Sweetie" until it drove us nuts. When we travelled together the Parrots would be transported back to Harrods for them to look after – they were best qualified to do so. I have no idea what the expense of the whole project was. From original purchase through to Harrods, 'kenneling', or whatever the term may be for Parrots, it must have been enormous. Quite an indulgence on Neil's part to satisfy a whim and his sense of humour – but I saw the funny side of the whole episode. Eventually, they were returned permanently to Harrods.

In late 1988 my oldest friend, Dianna Naylor, came to London. She was 'Miss Kenya' in the Miss World contest. She was also entered as 'Miss Africa'. The contest was held at the Albert Hall in November. Because of the strict security surrounding the whole contest, she wasn't allowed to stay with us overnight but we arranged to meet up a couple of times. I believe the girls always had to be accompanied by an approved companion or 'chaperone' for the duration of the competition and were not allowed to overnight elsewhere other than at the designated hotel.

By a strange twist of fate, one of the girls involved with the arrangements for her country's entrant turned out to be the Ethiopian girlfriend of Olav from Nairobi. Somehow during conversation we both realized who the other one was. She had no reason to bear me any animosity – as far as she was concerned I had looked after Olav's son whilst she was travelling, nothing more. I felt genuinely sorry for her but I could see nothing to be gained by either of us in my telling her how disgusting his behaviour had been towards me.

Dianna moved to London afterwards for a short while until her husband took a posting to the Turks and Caicos Islands for a time. They returned to London and we remain the closest of friends today.

In early 1989 news reached me from Kenya that my aunt was quite sick and it was suggested that I may want to consider visiting her sooner rather than later. Neil didn't hesitate: "You must go immediately," he said. He may have offered to accompany me, I can't remember, but I knew he was having a particularly busy time with his work and I wouldn't have pressed him to do so.

My 'big sister', cousin Khuleta, collected me at the airport and briefed me on the way about just how ill my aunt was. At least I was a little better prepared.

We arrived at my aunt's house on a Thursday or Friday to find many relatives gathered – confirmation, if any were needed, that the situation must be serious. There were cousins who I had almost forgotten about and others whose relationship I wasn't even sure of. But there was a houseful and there seemed to be a lot of squabbling going on amongst them. I paid little attention right then, I was there to see my aunt.

She was lucid but confined to her bed. We hugged and I was grateful to have the chance to talk to her alone for quite a long time. As she became weary she took my hand and with a smile she said, "I'm going home on Monday."

I spent most of my time at the house over the next couple of days, more often than not upstairs with the Giriama people. They always had a kind of spirituality about them that I found comforting and reassuring. On the Monday my cousin Mohammed came up to tell us that Mwana Kutani had passed peacefully away. We all cried and hugged one another.

Shortly afterwards my father arrived. I remember thinking: "Is there some significance in the fact that my aunt could wait for me to arrive from England before dying but she didn't wait for my father to arrive from Nairobi?" He entered, looked at me and as I approached, pushed me aside without a word and went to say farewell to my aunt. I returned to the roof to find that the squabbling between the relatives was in full flood. There were arguments about who should live in the house and who should have what. It was sickening to witness and all the while my aunt was lying on her deathbed beneath their feet, already being prepared for burial. Muslim burials are swift affairs.

We went down to be present as her body was removed from the house. They brought her into the living room passing the table where we had sat for our lunch throughout my childhood. For all the time I lived there I had no idea that the table had been placed over a disused well. As my aunt passed, so the entire covering of the well collapsed and the table lurched to one side. On one level it was startling but I smiled wryly inside at the thought that my aunt was having one last say about what she thought of the squabbling relatives.

For me, Mombasa would never be the same again.

Chapter Twenty

A few weeks before Christmas, 1989, Jack announced that he had booked for all of us to spend the whole of the festive season in Jamaica. As usual, no expense was spared and we enjoyed beautiful beachfront accommodation in stunning tropical surroundings. It was very romantic and I had long since overcome the hang-ups that led to us watching the boxing on our wedding night. I can't imagine what our relationship would have been like by then had Neil and I not been able to deal with that situation.

Shortly after our return to London we learned that I was pregnant with a due date of 18 October. I had conceived in Jamaica and we were thrilled to the point of tears. This time round we were sure of each other and as sure of our lives together as anyone can be. This time, bringing a child into our loving relationship was the most wonderful and most perfect thing imaginable. We were grateful too to be given another chance.

The flat at Pennybank Chambers had served us well and we had loved being there for four years or so. But it was too small to bring up a child and we started to look around.

Thomas Moore Street runs more or less parallel to the Thames behind St. Katherine's Dock down to Wapping. We loved the area for its convenience and its familiarity so we were delighted to find a redevelopment called 'Tradewinds', near Wapping High Street. We bought the 2-bedroom penthouse arranged over two floors. Bedrooms were en-suite and there was a spacious lounge and kitchen. We had a roof garden, a garage and further parking. The block was secure with a resident steward. It was a beautiful conversion, tastefully finished and with high ceilings. We were fortunate that we were financially able to move in right away without having to wait for the completion of the sale of our old flat.

When the funds from the sale did come through, Neil introduced me to a firm of interior designers based in Neal Street, Covent Garden. The apartment was amazing once they had finished with it.

I have very happy memories of sitting on the roof with Neil, a glass of wine in hand, watching the sunset over the Tower of London, the River, and the City beyond. It was a real oasis and our private space where no one and nothing in the world mattered but each other. If only time could stand still, frozen in such moments.

In May 1990 my father contacted me to say that he would be coming to London to visit my cousin who was sick. He asked if he could stay with us, to which Neil said, "Of course." Only then did we realize it would be the same time that we were due to fly to Berlin for a Coffee Traders Convention.

When my father arrived it was the first time we had met since he virtually disowned me at the time of my aunt's death in Mombasa. I collected him and Lydia, now his third wife, from Heathrow in my Porsche - not ideal but we managed. I had known Lydia as my father's girlfriend in Nairobi and some were surprised that he took her for a wife: Lydia was from the Taita tribe, traditionally Christian and often with fairer skin. Many looked upon them as possibly more beautiful than average but of a lower class. When my father announced his intention to take her for a wife, my stepmother, Rehema tried to make an ally of Aziza against her. But the two wives did not make good co-conspirators and Lydia became the main focus of my father's attention despite their efforts.

My mother must have been even more frustrated at the hand life had dealt her and the choices she had made. Certainly my father had been a bad move for her; most probably she would have been better off had she stuck with her first husband, Ahmed the butcher – he still brought her meat every day despite their divorce. Having an affair with, and then marrying my father hadn't worked out so well for her. The writing was pretty much on the wall very early on: she had been given the choice of the flat in Moons Cinema district, that Rehema then took, or the much smaller and less salubrious one she ended up with off Vanga Road.

Prior to that she had been living in a semi-detached place in

Kaloleni, not so far from Moons. When I say 'semi-detached' it was basically one building divided in a bit of a muddled way into two dwellings. (The other part of the house was occupied by a prolific and well known child-molester, a fact that didn't prevent people coming from miles around to buy his famous Samosas). But Aziza thought she could hold out for the place she really wanted, a house owned by my father with a small, fenced garden in the area of the Lighthouse. My father declined to let her live there and Vanga Road was all that was left.

We arrived, in my Porsche, at the gated entrance to Tradewinds, parked in the garage, and took the lift to our penthouse apartment. Although I hadn't seen my father to talk to since being ejected from his house in Nairobi, we had exchanged letters. I had told him about our travels and our lifestyle but I'm not sure he was convinced that even half of it was true. Now he could see that all of it was true, I hadn't been fantasising.

He said, "You've done very well for yourself, daughter", and he seemed genuinely happy for me. His reaction gave me the feeling that the rift between us may be healing. Perhaps I would be 'accepted back into the fold'. I was now expected to ask his forgiveness for everything I had done that may have earned his disapproval. In accordance with Swahili custom I knelt before him and kissed his feet. This I did without a moment's thought or hesitation, and he duly granted my absolution.

We agreed that he and Lydia should stay in our flat whilst we were in Berlin.

At the time I had two cousins who were ill – one in London with Leukemia, the other in Oman, badly injured in a car accident. That night I had a vivid dream that stayed with me long after I had awoken. In my dream Mwana Kutani visited me to tell me that the fate of my cousins was in my hands... but I could save only one of them. In the event, they both died and the dream haunted me long afterwards. By the time we returned from Berlin, my father and Lydia had departed.

Chapter Twenty-One

We entertained a lot at Tradewinds, sometimes in lavish style. I enjoyed hosting parties, formal and casual alike. Often the guests were commodity brokers who Neil worked or dealt with and many seemed to live in Essex. Only later did I hear the term 'Essex Girl', and I realised that some of the brokers' wives and girlfriends would probably have fitted the image of that particular epithet. To my recollection they were very genuine people and I liked and got on with them all.

At one time there was a train strike and to help ease their travel problems Neil invited one or two of them to stay over. Tradewinds was a very handy location for anyone working in the City. I never detected any hint of racism towards me with those people, although I was aware that racist remarks were commonplace at the time. In my experience with these acquaintances and in my work at the wine bar, racism didn't rear its head.

A lot of places we went to - dinners, receptions and the like - I would be the only black person in the room. But I never felt overawed or cowed because of it. My aunt's words stood me in good stead: "Always remember you have every right to be there – wherever you are."

The larger receptions and dinners, of course – such as those at the Grosvenor – were full of international guests from every nation but it made no difference to me even if I was the only non-white face in the room. I always made sure to watch and read the news so that I could discuss current affairs with a measure of confidence. I found that the majority of people I met had more intelligence than to pre-judge a person's opinion based on the colour of their skin.

With the latter weeks of my pregnancy came an easing-off of the hectic social life we had been leading – for me at least.

Thanks to Jack, a Harley Street obstetrician, who duly delivered my baby at the Portland Hospital, cared for me throughout. (He was in fact the second doctor to be engaged – I had declined to return to the first after judging his initial consultation and physical examination to be not at all appropriate).

On 18 October 1990, at the age of 24, I gave birth to my beautiful daughter, Syanne. In keeping with their custom, the Portland announced the birth in The Times. Neil was a very proud father; Jack a very proud grandfather.

Ann visited me in my private room at the Portland and opened with, "A shame it's a girl, our family usually has boys." Ann and her sister had only sons. Regardless of that opening remark, Ann has always been a loving grandmother to Syanne. As she was growing I made sure to take her to see Ann for a whole day every week so that they could bond. That bond is very strong to this day.

The best way I can describe Neil's reaction to Syanne's arrival is one of shock. He seemed stunned by her birth, taken off balance as though he was completely unprepared for the inevitable reality of it all. But he always was and is a wonderful father to her.

For the sake of practicality we sold the Porsche 924 and bought a Suzuki Vitara. The apartment soon transformed to suit the many needs of a growing baby.

When Syanne was about 6 months old I took her to Mombasa to introduce her to the family. Neil wasn't able to accompany me on that occasion but as usual I stayed at Nyali Beach. I took her to see Aziza and my Dad came to visit us at the hotel. He gave me six thousand Kenyan shillings in cash for Syanne. It was the most he had ever given me and I felt that the rift between us must truly be healed. I really had been forgiven and he felt a bond and grandfatherly responsibility for his granddaughter. All in all It was a good visit and it left me feeling that the circle had been completed.

For Syanne's first birthday we hosted a party. We bought an enormous clown cake from Selfridges and invited friends we had made with babies and children on the pretence that this was a party for the kids. Nonsense! It was as much for the adults and I made mountains of samosas and other tasty food from my youth.

Harvey's said they wanted me to keep working and such was the friendship and open-heartedness of Elke and Giovanni that they suggested I put Syanne in a play-pen behind the bar and simply carry on! I tried it for a week but decided that bringing up Syanne was more important in my life and hers. Neil readily agreed.

We arranged for a lady to come round on some mornings so that I could go to the gym. She took Syanne to some great places and always kept her very stimulated, as did we. We discovered many child-friendly places in London that we had not had reason to visit before. No more Greek nightclubs now!

Egon Ronay produced a guide to great eating-places such as Smolensky's. The waiters and waitresses dressed in a funky way and interacted with the kids. They served them the food they liked and the adults what they wanted.

The Arts Club in Dover Street became a favourite. We went to suitable exhibitions at museums and galleries. A child can have a very positive impact on their parents' lives in so many ways.

I sent my sister, Salma, a ticket and she flew over to be with us and help me with Syanne. She stayed about six months in our spare room and loved every minute of her time in London. Of course, thanks to Neil, she saw a side of London life that she would never have been able to afford. I was pleased that I could share our good fortune with her for a while. Of all my family, Husna and Salma remain my closest friends to this day. I would love to be able to make their lives worry-free if ever I have the chance. Both of them married and moved to Canada with their husbands and although they have a good life I would love to make it better.

In 1992 Neil and I started thinking that a thatched house in the country would be a better place to bring up children.

Great Dunmow in Essex is a very pleasant, rural location with some nice properties. We had known traders who lived in that area and loved it. We found more than one example of our perfect English Country Cottage with a thatched roof and small garden, not too large to manage. Neil said that although it was an idyllic setting, we would need to keep a flat in London: he had no desire to commute on a daily basis. This meant that I would be alone in the country with Syanne most of the week, most weeks. We agreed this dream needed a little more thought before committing to anything.

About that time Jack started talking about retiring, even though he was only in his mid-fifties. He had been very successful and a sale of his shares in the company had left him very comfortably off. Ann expressed concern about what he would do with himself if he did retire completely. Comments along the lines of, "I don't want you under my feet all day" and "what will you do, tend the roses all day?" were becoming commonplace. Jack wasn't sure what he was going to do either.

For Christmas '92 he booked a villa for the whole family in Barbados. Jack had a plan. Whilst we were there, unbeknown to any of us he had been looking around for a property to buy. He spotted "Lor Zonkel' owned by the Jockey, Scobie Breasley situated on the beach at Mullin's Bay, just south of Mullin's Beach Bar. He didn't hesitate.

After returning to the UK Jack started discussing the prospect of pruning roses in rainy England as against playing golf in the sun in Barbados. He quite clearly preferred the latter. At first Ann seemed to think it would be a holiday home where they might spend some months of the year. She was entitled to have come to that conclusion because they had recently bought and moved into a much more opulent house near RAF Northolt, not far from their old home in Pinner. Ann said she used to see the house as a child and had always aspired to live there one day. But now she realised that Jack was talking about relocating to Barbados on a permanent basis.

Although Jack invited Ann to join him, it seemed to me that he always knew he would be going without her. She seemed indifferent to that idea. In any case, she had her infirm mother to think about and she had her own circle of friends as well as the charity work she loved so much. At this point at least, both Jack and Ann seemed reconciled to the fact that they were about to go their separate ways.

But I wouldn't go so far as to say they were fully admitting it to themselves, let alone each other. They both knew, however, that for the most part their marriage was little more than a façade, a charade played out over many years for the sake of keeping up appearances.

The twist came when Jack suggested to Neil that he and I might like to think about trying the Barbados life for a year or two to see how things worked out. We could live with him and he would offer us a financial safety net until we could see what direction we wished to take. When Neil told me about it we agreed that we needed to think this through carefully. But it was a very attractive prospect.

We left Syanne in the capable care of our trusted sitter and headed for our favourite haunt, a place where matters of such importance could be given the proper attention.

Trader Vic's in the Hilton on Park Lane was funky, attracted the beautiful people of the time, and served great cocktails. We talked for hours and imbibed – perhaps a little too enthusiastically. Having taken all matters into consideration, including the suspension, if not termination of Neil's career, we decided it was an excellent idea, a faultless plan. As soon as Neil's speech was no longer affected by the cocktail intake, he would tell Jack we'd like to take him up on his suggestion.

From that point on, lunches at the Patterson's became somewhat strained. Ann felt betrayed; she could see her world crumbling. She now often referred to Jack breaking up the family and taking them away from her. And I think her resentment came as much from losing Syanne as it did from losing her son. Despite the state of her marriage, I think Ann, quite understandably, preferred the status quo.

I may have made our decision sound rather flippant and although we had Jack's support if we needed it, Neil and I were not naïve. From the moment we confirmed we would be going to Barbados we both knew that we would need to think about a plan for our future. And one idea was already hatching in our minds.

Chapter Twenty-Two

"Beautiful, beautiful Barbados"; the words of the song don't lie. It has the benefit of two distinctly different coastlines – the east constantly washed by Atlantic rollers and the west with its 'Platinum Coast' bathed by the calm, warm waters of the Caribbean. Let's not quibble about the official eastern limit of the Caribbean – to everyone who lives there and those who visit, this is the Caribbean.

The islanders have managed to create an extremely sophisticated and safe destination without losing their unique identity. I say unique because they are widely acknowledged to be the friendliest and most hospitable hosts throughout the islands. Here you will find world-class restaurants serving the finest cuisine anywhere, rubbing shoulders with Rum Shacks and little Chattel-House eateries offering peas and rice, chicken wings (or feet for the adventurous!) and 'pudding and souse'. The rich and famous, with the means to travel to anywhere their hearts desire, return to Barbados again and again, their perennial destination of choice. But the same is true of us lesser mortals - and we are made equally welcome. We moved there in the early summer of '93.

We had been extremely lucky with letting the apartment at Tradewinds to a Swiss banker on a two-year lease. This gave us an income sufficient to give us a good degree of independence in Barbados and we hadn't burnt our boats as far as the UK was concerned.

As I have said, a jockey previously owned the house in Barbados. Jack was over six feet tall. I don't recall all the alterations that were needed but the thing that sticks in my mind is that all the mirrors had to be moved higher.

Neil and I had been giving some thought to opening a gym, but the first year was one of pure hedonism. Jack and Neil obtained inshore boat driver licenses and Jack bought a speedboat. We spent a lot of time skiing or cruising the coast, stopping for a swim, pulling in somewhere for lunch; an idyllic life.

Early most mornings Jack would take himself off to play golf. He would often play a round on his own. Jack was content in his own company – in many ways a bit of a loner. I wondered how long he would be able to tolerate Neil, Syanne and me in his space. Sometimes he liked to potter in the garden and I think he still did a bit of business here and there.

Jack was a man of routine and he didn't take kindly to having his routine disrupted. He was pedantic in many things. After lunch he would take a siesta. On rising he would have a cup of tea and a smoke then take a swim. At six he would have a rum punch, either at home - the housekeeper made a potent version at her home and brought it in especially for Jack – or at Mullin's. After watching the sun go down, dinner would be served at 7pm. Lateness by others or anything disrupting his routine was a source of aggravation to Jack.

At the beginning of the week he would tell the cook what the menu was to be for the week. He did this every week for many weeks even though the cook knew that the menu was to be exactly the same as the week before. Eventually, Jack accepted that the cook could work this out for himself.

After a while this became too much for me and I began cooking curry dishes and other meals for Neil, Syanne and me to break up the monotony. I didn't pay attention to whether or not this rattled Jack in the same way other breaks with routine did but he seemed to enjoy my food when he joined us.

In the main, we all rubbed along together without much confrontation although Jack and I did clash at times. It was usually something quite trivial and we made up quickly. Jack was not a man to perpetuate an argument or bear grudges. Ann, however, could add another dimension. Even from a distance she managed to inject a certain amount of rancour between all of us. It was worse when she visited and I felt that she resented seeing us getting along together. Once again, I had sympathy with her position. Back in the family home in England, Ann definitely ruled the roost. Here in Barbados this was Jack's domain and it must have given Ann a feeling of redundancy to see him firmly in charge of his own domestic affairs. And Jack really did relish his newfound authority. This inevitably led to occasional friction: he was apt to forget from time to time that Neil and I were adults who had managed our own lives quite successfully prior to the current arrangements. He could sometimes treat us like unruly teenagers living at home.

Our son, Adam, was born 15 June 1994; I was 28 years old. Jack was once again the very proud grandfather but the strain of living under the same roof was beginning to tell on all of us. The arrival of a second child was never going to help.

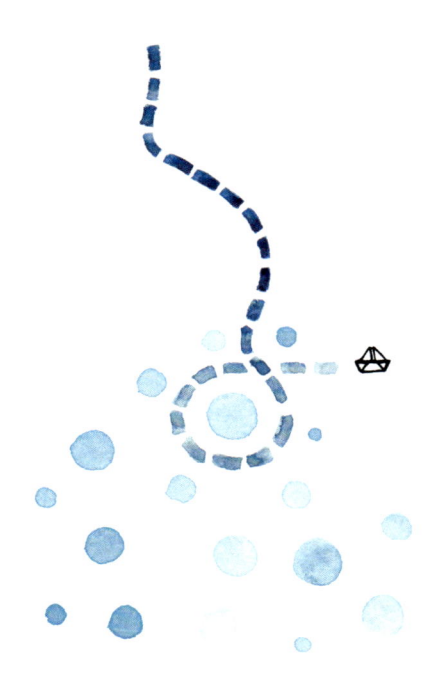

Although Neil and I had managed to produce Adam – and Neil was as delighted as me at his arrival – our relationship was tense. Even whilst we were still in London our intimacy was not all it should have been. If we had thought that Barbados would bring the spark back to our relationship, we were wrong. Neil spent long hours on his own in front of his computer. I occupied myself with the children and can't recall what else. We didn't talk very much.

Jack had different ideas about how we should raise the children, which put an even greater strain on the relationship between the three adults. For the first year we had the distraction of the daily beach life and the excitement of a new adventure in a tropical paradise. Most people of our age at the time would make the mistake of thinking that this way of life could be never ending. Even though we had realised from the start that we would have to think about earning a living at some time, it is easy to put the reality of life to one side when you are rapt by sun, sea, sand, Caribbean sunsets and rum-punch.

The Halcyon days of our first year or so in Barbados were drawing to a close and we all knew it.

Chapter Twenty-Three

It was probably quite soon after our arrival in Barbados that we had second thoughts about opening a gym. We didn't think it would be much of a money-spinner and it didn't give either of us a buzz. My training at Harvey's and my years of experience there meant that I was best qualified to continue in the hospitality sector. And anyway, I loved that business.

Neil had a brilliant mind for figures and superb organisational skills. A restaurant was now the plan but we wanted to feel our way on the Island before rushing into anything.

In late '94 I landed a job as front-of-house hostess at 'The Cliff', a new restaurant on the west coast. A huge investment had been put into the construction alone – the restaurant was virtually to hang off the cliff over the small beach below. It was tiered so that the maximum number of tables could have unobstructed views of the sea. No expense was spared in kitting-out the restaurant and kitchens and they wanted only the best staff available throughout. Neil took the job as Cashier.

The Cliff was destined to become the most prestigious dining venue in Barbados and it remains so today. The less formal Cliff Beach Club, recently built alongside on similar lines, compliments it perfectly.

At first we had babysitters coming to the house but Jack didn't like strangers in his space so that didn't last very long. He was such a giving man in so many ways and I will always be grateful to him for his boundless generosity. But Jack was punctilious in the extreme and a control freak – traits that Neil inherited. As both men have proved, these characteristics can make for success in business but on a domestic level they are teeth-grindingly difficult for others to endure.

We had to be at 'The Cliff', about fifteen minutes away, by 5.30pm so we dropped Syanne and Adam at the sitters thirty minutes before. We finished around midnight, picked the children up on the way home, and put them back to bed. It was far from ideal.

It wasn't long before we decided to go ahead with our own restaurant. We had our eye on a small bar called 'Ragamuffins', a few miles south of Mullins in Holetown. As well as drinks, they served some bar snacks but it seemed to us that it wasn't working to its full potential.

At the same time we spotted a plot of land in a wooded area called 'The Whim', near Speightstown, a few miles north of Jack's place. We sold 'Tradewinds' and bought both.

Neil left 'The Cliff' first in order to set up the restaurant. He did a great job when he set his mind to something and this was no exception. I followed shortly afterwards. We introduced a proper menu with 'Greek nights' and 'school dinners'. Neil and I worked very well together. Sometimes we approached business from different viewpoints, but our ideas were always very compatible.

Later, we employed three or four 'drag queens' who worked together. They would put on a show once a week and it wasn't long before word got round and the place was packed on those nights. A friend of mine had tipped us off that they were performing at a bar on the south coast and said we really should go and take a look. Neil and I decided we would go there on Valentine's night. They were incredibly good so we approached them and they agreed to work for us one night a week. They've continued to be a very popular attraction to this day.

We had encountered cross-dressing once before, during a trip to New York. A friend we had met there a couple of times invited us to be his guests at an event one doesn't attend every day: a dinner / convention for cross-dressers. I'd never experienced anything quite like it.

Hundreds of men attended with their wives or girlfriends (cross-dressing should not be confused with homosexuality), and we made up a pretty large contingent of guests who did not indulge in their particular predilection. I got to talk to some of the partners at length during the course of the evening. In many cases the men kept their activities secret from their other halves for quite some time. Friday night 'out with the boys' was a common deception. But 'the truth will out', and in the case of those in attendance that night, it was to the relief of both parties.

The ladies told me that, since it had become known to them, they would actively assist their partners with their make-up and dressing. They would go shopping together for gowns and shoes, make-up and accessories. Now, they would often go out together on a Friday as two females and I must say that some of the men looked more feminine and glamorous than their partners that night.

I had seen transvestites in Nairobi and they were often quite stunning but those attending this convention-cum-dinner were in a different league. I was surprised but not shocked. I'm not easily shocked and I never rush to judgement; they seemed happy and they were doing no one any harm.

Neil, too, is a very liberal, undiscriminating individual and we both found that we got along with the people there just fine.

During the first few months in Barbados, at a party one evening someone pointed to her friend across the room, a girl I didn't know. She told me that her friend's partner was having an affair but she couldn't bring herself to tell her. I said that I would certainly expect a true friend to tell me. This came back to haunt me.

Adam was a few months old when I received a call to say that Neil was messing around with someone else. He had been seen with her more than once and my friend was sure it wasn't innocent. I raised it with Neil and he denied it. Our marriage was already under pressure. Basically, Neil did his own thing while I was a mum to our kids. We were not really husband and wife and hadn't been for some time. Living in one room in Jack's house was not conducive to mending anything. In London we had been foolish to think that a change of climate and scenery would improve things. I'm not sure either of us really believed it but I'm certain we were neither the first nor the last to ignore the facts in this way.

Jack knew that Neil was 'playing away from home' and they had a big argument. Quite ridiculously, at one point Jack said that if Neil didn't 'tow the line' he would send him back to England. It was ludicrous but it didn't surprise me that Jack would say such a thing – he saw us as kids, not adults. The situation deteriorated further until we had an enormous row about, well, I don't know what it was about, but it was the final straw and we moved to a flat. Our house was still being built.

If I were reading this account, by now I would be asking some questions about the sanity of this couple. With their marriage quite obviously on the rocks they were building a house and going into business together! What on earth were they thinking? It seems quite odd, I know. But we didn't hate each other and I think we just kept going through the motions. I don't remember over-thinking the whole subject of the house or the restaurant. In fact, I can only remember each of us being excited about the prospect of both.

We loved our children and I'm not saying that we stayed together just because of them but we seemed to have a lot more binding us together than was tearing us apart.

We called the house 'Tsavo', after the Kenyan game reserve. I had designed it along the lines of my father's house in Kitale; I had very fond memories of my times there. It was built on stilts so that our dogs could sleep under and we had a table tennis table on the large patio. It was practically a replica of my dad's place.

In May 1999, whilst all this turmoil was happening, I received a phone call from my sister, Husna. She was sobbing but saying nothing comprehensible. I began asking her who had died because it was evident that someone had. I concluded that it must be either Mum or Dad.

"Who's died?" I said. "Is it Mum or is it Dad?"

She eventually managed to tell me that my Dad had passed away in hospital in Nairobi. A few days earlier he had been taken there by my brother, Mohammed and now he had succumbed. Apparently, he hadn't suffered. I was never prepared for how I would feel with the passing of either my father or my mother but now, phone in hand, I cried with my sister.

Syanne and Adam were both there when I broke down and I told them their grandfather had passed away. They were not close to him and it didn't affect them in the way it did when Jack passed away, ten years later. They were much closer to him and his passing was much more poignant for them and possibly for all of us. We loved him very much and he'd always been so good to us all.

But now they empathized with my sadness at the passing of my father, hugged me, and shed a tear too. Although we had made our peace that time in London, Dad and I were never all that close. Nevertheless, it is sad to lose a parent and it did upset me in that moment, perhaps more than I was expecting. But I didn't dwell on it, accepted it as part of the circle of life, and moved on.

When finally we moved into the house, our marriage had deteriorated further. We had both been pretending for a long time. Intimacy was now practically non-existent. Neil suggested that we should face the reality of our situation and lead separate lives. I agreed it was for the best. Oddly enough, despite this arrangement we worked very well together as colleagues and co-owners of 'Ragamuffins'. No one would have guessed there was anything wrong with our marriage and the business flourished.

At weekends, the children would often go to stay with Jack. He was a very good grandfather and the situation worked well for him and for the children – he had control of the situation without our input and that was the way he functioned best. They loved their weekends with him.

Neil and I really did take our 'separate lives' arrangement seriously, or so it seemed at first. On Friday nights, after closing the restaurant, I would join some girlfriends at a nightclub or jazz venue, usually at one of the resorts on the south coast. Neil invariably stayed at home doing whatever it was he did on his computer.

In theory, we should both be happy with the deal but Neil often acted like a moody, jealous husband although there were no grounds for his jealousy. I usually returned home around 4 am, the last to be dropped off by the cab that my friends and I shared home. Some ugly scenes started to develop – never in front of the children – and I began to feel genuinely scared by Neil's behaviour. One time in particular he became extremely menacing. He was not a bad man, far from it, but his controlling nature meant that his mind could not cope with this radical pact with his own wife.

Jack was well aware of our situation. He won a weekend at Almond Beach, an all-inclusive resort, and he gave it to us, hoping it may help. We arrived on Friday night to be greeted by the local press and the competition organisers. There were several other couples that had won this romantic weekend for two. All couples were wearing matching T-shirts showing how united and 'loved-up' we all were. Neil and I found it amusing knowing where our relationship was at that time. For the sake of the cameras and the interviewer, however, we were the perfect married couple.

When they had finished their work, we went to our venue of choice: Mullin's. I hadn't planned it but I suddenly heard myself saying that I wanted a divorce.

Neil said calmly, "Oh, OK."

It felt like a weight had been lifted off both our shoulders. We practically celebrated, had more drinks and then went on somewhere for more afterwards. On Saturday morning, however, Neil was in a very black mood. He said, "OK, now we really do lead separate lives." And he left me there.

On the Saturday night, Jack brought the kids and we all stayed over. Neil and I kept up the usual pretence for the sake of the children.

Any intimacy that had remained – as rare as it was – finally died completely and we agreed that we should go for counseling. The counsellor asked us in turn why we were there. I said something like, "To deal with the fact that our marriage is over." Neil said, "To mend our broken marriage." This did not bode well and I knew this was going nowhere, even if Neil wasn't yet ready to admit it.

But Neil was not a stupid man. He did face up to it and moved out. Now we really did lead separate lives. Nonetheless, we continued to work well together and Ragamuffins thrived.

Syanne was doing well at school and Adam was about to start too. I will always be grateful to Jack for seeing them both through to their eleven-plus. He was a good man. He covered their fees at good schools and Neil and I covered any extras and trips fifty-fifty.

In 2000, Neil and I were divorced.

Chapter Twenty-Four

Our divorce was very amicable. The first lawyers I approached said, "We'll milk him for every penny." I dropped them immediately. We then engaged a brother and sister team, each representing one of us. They were meticulous about ensuring there was no conflict of interest but they were prepared to pay attention to the fact that they were there to implement in law what Neil and I had already agreed between us.

Up to the time that Neil moved out, I don't think his family knew how serious our situation had become. Maybe they thought living separate lives under the same roof was normal – Jack and Ann had managed it for years without ever considering divorce. But when it came to the moment that it was obvious we were divorcing, I think Neil's family thought the best solution was to buy me off so that I couldn't take the children. I never intended to do that, but I think they were used to throwing money at any given situation, even if they only feared the worst.

In fact, the court awarded me outright custody but I immediately shared it with Neil. I despise couples that use their children as weapons in divorce proceedings.

Jack stopped talking to me for quite a while afterwards.

I loved Neil on a different level now, more like a trusted friend or perhaps a favourite brother. On reflection, our relationship had probably returned to being what it always had been - what it should have remained. But we had two beautiful children and for that reason alone I would do the whole thing over again. I would gladly take all the pain again just to have my two kids.

Immediately after the divorce, Neil and I were quick to tell the children that it had nothing to do with them and that we both loved them. We have always showed that to them and I don't believe there is any doubt in their minds about it.

Having said that, Neil had, for some years, been quite withdrawn into himself and he was not very engaging with the children. He was always a good provider but he did not give of himself emotionally until after the divorce. From then on I think he realised and regretted the time he had lost but he changed dramatically and I cannot fault him as a father to his kids now. It's never too late to mend.

I hope I've been a good mother.

The terms of the divorce meant that I now had full responsibility for the running of 'Tsavo'. Neil sat with me and showed me the bills that had to be paid; I was shocked. But I was determined to make it work.

Neil said, "If you save money and watch what you spend, you will make it ok."

He paid only a hundred Barbados dollars – about fifty US or thirty GB Pounds – per week for each child. This was the amount offered by the lawyer and even though it was inadequate, I never argued for more. But Neil would never have seen the children come to harm or really want for anything.

I was very proud of the mature way that Syanne and Adam understood that there were things they simply couldn't have. They fully appreciated that I needed to watch the pennies now. All my credit cards were stopped and I destroyed them. What embarrasses me most looking back is the bank manager gently pointing out to me that when you write a cheque, there needs to be money in the account to clear it. I had never needed to think about this crucial detail since my arrival in England with Neil.

Jack was talking to me again and he very generously paid to have the whole house decorated.

Dad left me about fifty thousand Barbados Dollars which cleared all my debts and credit cards. It also enabled me to undertake some much needed maintenance on 'Tsavo'. I replaced some flooring with more expensive wood and renewed some tiling. It was important to me that Syanne and Adam's childhoods were disrupted as little as possible by the divorce. With their parents and grandparents behaving in a civilized manner with one another, I think we achieved that.

Neil's and my relationship was better now than it had been for years.

The 5th of April 2006 was my 40th birthday and I took the kids to Puerto Rica. Neil and I had enjoyed a trip there some years earlier. I was doing ok in my work and I was proud I could do it. The divorce settlement meant that, whilst I kept 'Tsavo', Neil kept Ragamuffins, and I ceased to work with him. I had considerable experience in the hospitality industry by now and I had built a good reputation for myself in Barbados. I had risen to manage various restaurants on the island. I also started to do some interior design and some wedding planning.

The British comedian and presenter, Bob Monkhouse originally had the house on the beach next to the 'Lone Star' restaurant where I was now manager. Shortly before he died he sold it and bought a property in a gated community at Sugar Hill, a little inland. His widow, Jackie, explained that he knew she didn't feel safe alone in the house on the coast. She saw how I decorated the restaurant for Christmas and loved it so much she asked me to do her house for her.

It was her first Christmas without her husband and she wanted her home decorated because she was going to have her grandchildren to visit. She wanted to make it special so we sat together to discuss the design. She decided she wanted traditional green, red and gold, and I had a timeline. I set to work and got Syanne and Adam to help me, but they were quickly bored with the task. But I made the timeline and Jackie was very pleased with the result. She also asked me to take care of taking it all down afterwards.

I discovered that I had an artistic flair that I hadn't been aware of till then. We spoke at some length during the arrangements and I felt privileged to meet her. She shared some of her books with me and it was obvious how much she loved her husband. It was very sad that she, too, passed away the following year.

I was engaged to organise weddings in every last detail. Others asked me to design and fit out their homes. Such commissions could earn me ten thousand dollars sometimes. I had made things work for me since the divorce and I'd taken good care of my kids.

I could see my life settling into a pattern now and I quite liked the look of the future that lay ahead of me. I decided to try to make amends with my mother so I sent her a ticket to come and stay with me in Barbados. She had been once before, whilst Neil and I were still married. It really hadn't gone well. On that occasion I tried to tell her how rejected I felt by her as a child and indeed, ever since. She became very defensive and was in complete denial about her treatment of me so I dropped it. She wasn't an evil woman, just a selfish one. But I did understand that she had her own disappointments to cope with.

This time it was just her, the children, and me and I really felt quite optimistic about her visit. It went worse than the first time. We had something new to fall out over – she began disciplining Syanne for what I saw as no good reason. And all the old issues rumbled on alongside the new ones.

She had cataracts and really couldn't see too well at all. It sounds wicked, I know, but I was grateful she had not had them dealt with at the time: it meant that she could not see the small tattoo I had – a sun on my right leg above the ankle. The sun represents light – the meaning of the name Nur in Arabic, Nuru in Swahili. Thinking varies about the reason that tattoos are not acceptable in Islam. Some say that it is a form of deception, others that it is bodily mutilation – the changing of Allah's creation. Some talk of it inflicting unnecessary pain and it may surprise you to learn that this is frowned upon in Islam. Whatever the reason, tattoos are not normally tolerated.

As a child I was obviously made aware of this and I always wondered why so many of the Yemenis could have such fancy art on their faces. I thought perhaps it was Henna but it seemed to be permanent. I never did find out the reason this was permitted and I suppose my lack of interest in religion meant that I didn't try too hard to do so.

My mother and I parted on reasonable terms, regardless of our differences. I'm happy for that because I was destined never to see her again.

Links with my family had faded over the years except with my sisters, Husna and Salma. I love them dearly and they have always returned that love unreservedly.

Whilst I was still living at Jack's, my younger brother, Mohammed, came to stay. I had little love for Mohammed. He and Jack got on well and drank together. He came a second time and I liked him even less. As a child, Mohammed was always rude, arrogant, and aggressive, especially towards us girls. If you so much as touched him, perhaps by brushing past, he would hit you hard and claim that it was his right to do so. He drinks freely and shows no sign of charity towards others, one of the Five Pillars of the faith of which he claims to be such a devout follower. Later, I visited him at his home in Vancouver and found his behaviour towards me so vile that I packed and left to stay at a hotel without saying a word.

Mohammed is a compulsive liar and a hypocrite. I hope never to see him again and I would not want him to have any influence over my children.

In July 2006 I had a call from Husna. This time, although she way crying, she clearly told me that our mother had died. We cried, agreed we were going to miss her, and wished each other well. I knew my mother had been unwell. I remember calling Kenya to talk to her; it was hard for her to speak and it got worse. I called again and this time she couldn't come to the phone. I knew in my heart she didn't have long for this world.

I can say that I had made peace with my parents and have no regrets. Nor do I fear my own death; we will all pass that way one day.

I moved on with my emotions and I realised that never again would I have the same urge to return to the country of my birth.

Later that same summer, Neil said that Ann had seen a challenge she thought he might like to take on: a trek in Nepal to Everest Base Camp for charity for children with cerebral palsy. We had both enjoyed less ambitious trekking in various locations over the years and he asked me if I'd like to go too. The trek was due to take place in November and it would mean that I would need to be away for about three weeks for the two-week trek. November is the start of the high season in Barbados and the most inconvenient time to lose your Restaurant Manager.

Christian Roberts is a charming, kind man and the Lone Star was his baby. He was an excellent employer who was generous and always very supportive of his staff. With his blessing, Rory, the General Manager for the Hotel and Restaurant, approved my leave. Although he must have been concerned about the timing he said, "Don't worry, we will work something out." Now I had to think about who would look after the kids.

Neil had a girlfriend who he said would help out as much as she could. Ann would come over and she and Jack would also help. Between them, they would manage and the kids would be well looked after.

Neil's girlfriend was very nice and incredibly understanding. They subsequently married and had a child together. Not only was she allowing him to go away with his ex-wife for three weeks - sharing a tent - but she would help to look after his children into the bargain. That should have been enough for me. But I got myself in a knot about being a protective mother and suchlike. I don't think jealousy entered into the equation, but I can't be sure. By the time we were on the flight to London, Neil and I weren't talking. Fortunately, all was healed by the time we boarded the onward flight to Doha. The way in which we fell out and made up again so quickly was typical of the tiffs we had during our marriage. That much hadn't changed.

Chapter Twenty-Five

The trek in Nepal was an amazing experience. We flew from London Heathrow on 24th November 2006 with Qatar Airways to Doha. I was very impressed by the airline staff as well as the food and I thought that this was an airline I wouldn't mind using again. But my affection for things Qatari ended there.

I have little to say about our stop at Doha except that I was surprised to find that I really didn't like the place. I thought that I might, seeing how familiar I was with Islamic society. But Doha bore no resemblance to Mombasa and I really didn't like it. I wondered how I might feel about other destinations in the Middle East.

We met with our fellow trekkers there. I didn't know what to expect; perhaps a lot of strong, mountaineering types with all the kit and a wealth of experience - and me, the novice outsider. But almost immediately I realised they were all just ordinary people like me with a thirst for a challenge. I was relieved not to feel intimidated. I introduced myself to John from Norfolk and another guy called Mike. Then there was Chris - he had climbed Kilimanjaro.

In the plane for our onward flight to Nepal I sat with John who was passionate about cooking and had a background in construction. It made for a good flight and I felt elated to be on my way with a bunch of nice people around me.

When we landed, the reality of where we were and what we were about to do kicked in and I wasn't ready for the emotion of it all. I boarded the bus for the hotel with tears in my eyes. The streets were buzzing with little motorbikes everywhere. There were hundreds of them and it was difficult to work out if there was any real traffic system – it just seemed like chaos. But somehow it worked. Some of the maneuvers were shocking but they seemed to get away with it. The hodgepodge of carts, motorbikes, bicycles, and people made a fascinating sight, really quite beautiful to see first hand.

We had supper together at the hotel and the next morning

attended the briefing by the team leaders. They told us the rules and regulations, which we must adhere to, and gave us some bits of advice gained from years of experience. At the end of the briefing they read out a poem written by the mother of a child with cerebral palsy. It was heart-rending and gave us all the feeling that this thing had to be done. I thought, "We are here to help this charity and we're blessed to have the opportunity as well as the physical ability to do so."

Before that, though, they hit me with the bit I had been dreading: during the trek we would be crossing eight suspension bridges of the flimsy, swaying side-to-side kind. As I discovered to my abject horror, some of these were not secured as well as they might have been. I got a great sense of achievement out of conquering my fear to deal with those bridges. In reality, I had no choice other than to do so. But it still felt so good each time I reached the other side, and not just for the relief I felt standing on solid ground once more.

After the briefing we had a day tour of Katmandu. In Dunbar Square we saw beautiful children begging and it made me sad and grateful that my children were safe and had a good home. We visited temples and browsed the market where I bought a fine Pashmina and some trinkets.

The next morning we took a light plane to Lukla from where we were to start our trek. Our Sherpas, who met us at Lukla, were so friendly and welcoming. They seemed such happy people despite the hard life they had to endure to put food on the table.

I remember Angshery in particular. During the trip he helped me a lot with my pack especially when I developed a bad cough or if I was feeling lethargic. When the trek was over I gave him my warm clothes, boots and gloves and some cash. They are fantastic people and they have so little. One of the greatest enemies on such adventures is the ever- present threat of dehydration. It can creep up on you without you being aware of it. You put in such an effort concentrating on the trail, where you are placing your feet, where your fellow trekkers are – everything except the fact that you are getting thirsty. By the time you realise, it can be too late. And it's not just a case of suddenly drinking lots of water to put it right – by then you've already started losing electrolytes and it can be a slow process getting back to the right levels. Dehydration will slow you down much more efficiently than any blister. Its onset was further hastened towards the latter part of the trek when I contracted a stomach bug.

On most nights the temperature dipped to minus 15C. The combination of all these factors, along with the relentless daily exertion, was quite exhausting. We were divided into two groups. The weaker ones (including me) would leave around 6am and trek for eight hours. The stronger group could cover the same ground in a shorter time and left later.

If Neil's girlfriend did have any worries about him sharing a tent with his ex wife, she needn't have: quite apart from the exhaustion, we really did seem to look upon each other like brother and sister. Perhaps this tells better than anything else the reason why our marriage didn't work out.

Neil and I were supportive of each other but individually determined to be as strong as any other member of the team. Each member was similarly resolute and it made for a good trek with a deep-seated camaraderie.

At one point we managed to visit the Edmond Hilary Clinic where we met an amazing doctor. This man had the opportunity to work in Harley Street but instead decided he could do more good here, helping his own people. You just had to have massive respect for the man.

Our Sherpas and all the Nepalese we met were marvelous, generous-hearted people. We also liked and got on well with our fellow trekkers - important on such a venture when you never know who you may have to call on for help along the way. The mountains, the people, our Sherpas and the team – I found the whole experience very humbling. It made me very aware of how small and insignificant we all are.

One evening Neil told me that after our divorce he had gone to London and whilst there he looked up an old girlfriend who he invited to join him for dinner. He must have come to the conclusion that all relationships can go from intimacy to being just good friends. Apparently, she had waited, unmarried for all those years and now that he was free again she assumed that they would wed. (I think Ann might have preferred it had Neil married her in the first place.) When he told the girl that there was absolutely no question of them marrying and that he had just called her for old-time's sake, she was devastated. She fled the restaurant leaving Neil in a totally bemused state. I felt sorry for the poor girl but I just had to laugh: he could be such an innocent at times. And he had no idea about the thinking processes of the female of the species.

We completed the trek without incident and I raised a decent amount for my children's charity. I think for both of us it was like closing a chapter and we returned to Barbados the best of friends and content in our minds that this was the best way for us to remain.

Chapter Twenty-Six

At the time of writing I am entering my fifty-first year. During the time around April 5th 2016, I celebrated my fiftieth with friends local to Barbados and some who travelled here to join me. I'm particularly happy to say that Husna and Dianna were amongst them.

My partner, Tony, with whom I've lived for a number of years, organised several events over almost a week. Some bits were quite elaborate and some down to earth - the way I find most people like to spend their time on our beautiful island. Tony's work and my own often have elements of crossover: he may be overseeing the renovation, ongoing maintenance and security of a property while I am organising the housekeeping and domestic arrangements. We work well together. But we also work completely independent of each other. Tony has added a new dimension to my life and I am so grateful for the immense effort he put into the arrangements for my birthday. His organisational skills are second to none, honed, no doubt, during his time as a Colonel in the Royal Marines. He also has the very best contacts and there could be no one better to arrange a week of celebrations for a special birthday.

Partying started with a casual get-together at Mullin's one evening where most of the overseas visitors met and got to know each other before the 'main event'… or events. Tony then chartered a party boat called the 'Buccaneer' for a run up the west coast with music, rum punch, food, dancing and swimming. That was a crazy five hours!

On the Saturday night we held a party at a property Tony looks after for the owners. We had a marquee, a great local band and 170 guests for a seated dinner. It went on into the small hours.

On my birthday the following Tuesday we took 10 close friends to dinner at the Cliff Beach Club. By the following morning we were well and truly 'partied out'.

But it was a great week and I really appreciated all the work Tony had put into making it so.

On the morning of my birthday he brought me tea in bed – not an unusual thing for him to do – and gave me my present. It was a diamond and emerald ring. I asked him which finger I should put it on and he said, "The second finger of your left hand."

I said, "Does this mean it's a 'promise ring'? Are we engaged?"

He replied, "Take it how you want. But I would love you to wear it all the time."

That sounds very much like a 'Tony Proposal' to me. I never expected him to go down on one knee!

So he has finally committed to me – but there is the small matter of his divorce, which he is apparently dealing with. For this reason, we are keeping our engagement low-key for now although the Island is like a village; I'm sure anyone who's interested – and many who are not - know about the ring. Some will claim to have known even before Tony thought of the idea!

I was always looking for my 'knight in shining armour'; at the age of 50 I hope I have found him. It's another milestone in my life and I'm excited about the adventure going forward.

Returning for a moment to the matter of my 'Party Week': 170 guests does sound an awful lot of people to know well enough to invite to your fiftieth. A large contingent was made up of Tony's ex-army / Marine friends and their wives. Others were people we have dealt with, worked with or become acquainted with in Barbados over the years. My daughter, Syanne, and my son Adam were also there. They were, of course, the most important ones to have with me. In reality, however, I don't have a need to 'collect' friends. I have enough friends and it's nice to meet people and to have them as acquaintances. But I don't need hoards of people to call 'friends'. Sometimes people don't know how to take me. I like people to tell the truth and I, in turn, like to tell it the way it is. I am not given to 'sugar-coating' the facts. Some people don't like to hear it that way.

Perhaps I shouldn't always be so forthright; perhaps some people really can't handle it.

Whatever the future holds, I am very proud of the way that Neil and I have brought up our children. I always gave them a good home, fed them well and gave them very strong values. With Jack's help, we saw them both through a good education.

Syanne got her Bachelor of Arts degree from Central St. Martin's in London and a first class honours in Graphic Design. During her time at university she started doing some modeling and in March 2016 she was signed by an agency in Cape Town, a place she loves. Together with her other signings, this means that she is now appearing on the covers of some very prestigious publications.

Adam also has the artistic flair that I would like to think is at least partly due to my genes – even if I didn't realise I had those genes before my time in Barbados. He also attends Central St. Martin's and will graduate next year. He has taken a gap year to do work assessment in Rotterdam.

Apart from the money left to cover their university, Jack also left them some funds in trust until their 25th birthday as a start in life. I have no idea how much it is but I know Neil will take good care of that situation for them.

Syanne turned 25 last year.

A couple of weeks after the birthday celebrations the world learnt of the premature death of the artist, "Prince" and it brought memories of my days in Nairobi flooding back: the DJ at 'Carnivore' always played great music and a firm favourite of mine was 'When Doves Cry', by Prince. If the DJ didn't play it, I or someone else would request it, and I would dance and sing along, euphorically.

I've been very lucky in life and always managed to make my way somehow. For me, the glass is always half full. I'm not afraid of hard work and I give a hundred percent to anything I undertake. So the future holds no fears for me; I'm grateful for my life so far. And having such wonderful children is the blessing for which I am most thankful. My proudest achievement is their upbringing, their values and what they have become. I hope I will be around for many years to watch them blossom into the beautiful human beings I know they are.

Epilogue

As Nuru prepared to celebrate her 50th Birthday, American drones and airstrikes hit an Al Shabaab training camp in Somalia killing, it was claimed, at least one hundred and fifty terrorists-in-training.

Offshore, a coalition warship intercepted a vessel carrying arms from Oman, allegedly destined for those same terrorists.

In Mombasa a young man sat on the ground, his back against the wall on the outskirts of the Old Town. His eyes were bloodshot and unseeing, his trousers urine-soaked. He remained only half upright, leaning on one elbow. He is one of many victims of the latest activity to thrive in this jewel on the Swahili Coast.

Mombasa is once again at the heart of trade in the Northern Indian Ocean. This time, however, the Swahili may not be so keen to claim their mercantile dominance in the region. But the trade in narcotics cannot be attributed solely to them, although they may count some of the traffickers in their number.

Nuru's old fellow pupil Ahmed and his cousin Ali meet on Saturday lunchtimes. They may take tea and perhaps a snack at 'Hoteli', the little café on the edge of Old Town. Their lives, however, are more complex than in those early days when they would meet on Fridays at the Mosque with their fathers. They often reflect on the relative simplicity of those times.

Ali has his own import and export business whilst Ahmed graduated from the University of Nairobi to be the first in his family to go on to medical school in London becoming a paediatrician. As part of his studies he spent time in some fine hospitals both in Kenya and overseas. But he decided to put what he took as his good fortune, to use in the service of the people of his own nation.

Ahmed and Ali pray where and when they can. Many around them are in the same position. What neither of them manages on a regular basis is to attend Friday prayers. They have, in any event, long

Epilogue

since ceased attending the Masjid Musa of their younger days. The strident rhetoric there became too much for both of them.

Somewhat ironically, although they had been exposed to the radicals in their own community it was during his time at medical school in London that Ahmed encountered some of the most vociferous extremists. Some were fellow students but the worst came in as guest speakers. He found he had no more in common with those people than he had with the ones who did their best to poison minds in Mombasa.

Before moving to Nairobi, Ali's stepbrother, Omar, twenty-seven years his junior, did continue to attend the Mosque. In recent years, Ali had made regular attempts to steer Omar away from the sphere of influence of the more highly charged elements there.

In September 2013, Ali and Ahmed contrived to include Omar in their meeting at the café, both of them fearing that he was making some poor life choices. But Omar did not appear. They hardly noticed because, along with all the other customers in the café and many passers-by, their attention was focused on the small TV set that sat on a high shelf above the serving bench at the back of the café. What they were witnessing filled them with horror. For the first time, thanks to live TV, they had a front row seat as the ghastly events at the Westgate Shopping Mall in Nairobi unfolded.

They returned to the TV set, any TV set, at every possible moment over the coming days, each time with still less comprehension of what was being enacted before their eyes, in their country, by people about whose ideology they had no concept, still less empathy.

Omar's family were never to see him again. Nor did they ever discover what became of him. They struggled to comprehend the rumours.

The Swahili children of Mombasa were always free to make their own choices in life. Some may have believed they could secure their place in Jannah by following the misdirection of the radicals.

It is difficult for most right-thinking people to believe that Paradise awaits those who slaughter others. The majority remained faithful to Islam and could see the true meaning of the tenets of that faith. They may have become doctors or entrepreneurs and contributed positively to their society.

One chose to turn her back on all religion, whilst retaining the utmost respect for those who did adhere to whichever faith they chose to follow. Paradoxically, she conducted her life according to the best laws laid down by many faiths - including Islam. Her early upbringing in the House within the Stone Walls in Mombasa Old Town had instilled in her solid values rather than blind faith. Through her determination to pass those values on to her children, the influence of Mwana Kutani, and her enlightened father before her, lives on.

End

Read Omar's story in *Omar*

Available in Summer 2017

"He had been sitting alone in the darkness for several hours contemplating his lot. As he looked down at the stump where his left leg used to be he wondered how he had arrived at this point in his life. In his depressed state of mind he reasoned that he might not have reached his nadir; there could easily be worse to come."